Waiting for the Mountain to Move:
And other Reflections on Life

D0121969

ALSO IN ARROW BY CHARLES HANDY

The Age of Unreason

WAITING FOR THE MOUNTAIN TO MOVE

And other Reflections on Life

Charles Handy

ARROW

First published in Arrow 1992

3 5 7 9 11 12 10 8 6 4 2

© Charles Handy 1991

First published in 1991 by Hutchinson

Arrow Books Limited
Random House UK Ltd, 20 Vauxhall Bridge Road, London SW1V 2SA

Random House Australia (Pty) Limited
20 Alfred Street, Milsons Point, Sydney,
New South Wales 2061, Australia

Random House New Zealand Limited
18 Poland Road, Glenfield
Auckland 10, New Zealand

Random House South Africa (Pty) Limited
PO Box 337, Bergvlei, South Africa

Random House UK Limited Reg. No. 954009

A CIP catalogue record for this book
is available from the British Library

ISBN 0 09 983080 9

Printed and bound in Great Britain by
Cox & Wyman Ltd, Reading, Berkshire

Contents

v

Contents

Contents

DEDICATION

To the memory of Robert Foxcroft

ACKNOWLEDGEMENTS

Every writer needs a benevolent critic, every broadcaster a producer, and every author a publisher. I have been lucky enough to have had all these to help these reflections take shape.

Elizabeth is my benevolent critic. Because she is also my wife and my business partner she knows only too well when I am being less than genuine. I am more grateful than she believes for her patience, honesty and encouragement. Robert Foxcroft was my first producer of the BBC talks. I was fortunate; fortunate too in his successors, Beverley MacAinsh, John Newbury and Chris Morgan. They coach me over the telephone, just to prove that you can have wonderfully productive relationships with people you never meet. Gail Rebuck is my publisher. Her enthusiasm, imagination and efficiency make it all possible, and exciting.

I thank them all.

By Way of Introduction

'Would you like to do a "Thought"?' asked Robert Foxcroft one day. I knew what he meant and, because I knew, was both flattered and surprised. 'Thought' was short for 'Thought for the Day', a three-minute religious reflection slotted in between the news headlines and the weather every morning on the BBC's early morning radio programme *Today*. Robert was the producer. It was that question of Robert's which, years later, gave birth to this book of reflections or thoughts.

The god-slot, as 'Thought for the Day' was popularly known, was conventionally filled by bishops, priests and rabbis and I was none of those. But I was known to Robert who acted as producer of this one daily spot as well as being vicar of St Peter's Church in Hammersmith, London. Robert felt that I, as a rather renegade professor of business with theological affinities, might relate particularly to the many thousands of business and professional people who regularly tuned in to this programme.

1

'Actually,' said Robert, 'a few million people are listening, but don't get conceited, they won't have tuned in to listen to you. Half of them are in their cars and use the programme to distract them from the thought of the day ahead, the others are naked in their bath or using the radio for wallpaper sound or an alarm clock as they go about their early morning chores. Your task is to say something interesting so that they really start to listen.'

I was, as I said, flattered. The first 'Thought' was scheduled for months ahead. I had a holiday in Provence looming up and I planned to use it to polish my ideas. I came back with some sample scripts. Robert read them carefully. 'Yes,' he said, 'they're about right for length, but, well, this is supposed to be *A* Thought for *the* Day, not the encapsulated wisdom of a lifetime. Ideally, it needs to relate to something that's happening in the news or in your own life, a little nugget to chew on as they go to work.' I tore them up and started again – or rather I learned not to start on them until the day before so that they really would be fresh and relevant.

Robert, sadly, died not long afterwards, to leave a huge gap in the lives of his many friends. I shall forever be grateful to him because he made me think, think about what mattered to me in life, think about my beliefs, such as they were and how they came about, think particularly about how those beliefs shed light on the countless dilemmas and worries that seemed to make up the workaday world of myself and people like me.

Three minutes, 540 words or so. It doesn't sound much, but it's the most difficult thing I ever have to do and in many ways the most rewarding – when and if it comes right. It is a great privilege to be allowed to share your personal beliefs with millions of others, whether they're listening or not, to be given three minutes with no interruptions, no questions asked, no editing. The presenters in the studio have no warning or knowledge of what I'm going to say and the rules are that they must let me say it. I sometimes wonder what would happen if I abandoned my script and started to hurl abuse at the BBC, the Prime Minister or the Queen, calling down upon them the wrath of God. Would anyone then interrupt?

Most of these reflections are slightly edited versions of those early morning 'Thoughts'. Some arose from other occasions. They spread over five years, five years which saw the end of the Cold War and the start of a Gulf War. Five years which, nearer home and the lives of most of us, saw stock markets and housing markets boom and burst, earthquakes in San Francisco and hurricanes in unusual places like southern England; but five years, too, which saw the ups and downs of life in home and office continue as they have always done, whatever happens in the big world outside.

My task, as I saw it, was to look for the meaning and the moral in those happenings, if there was one, and to put them all to the test of my beliefs. Sometimes I have thought that everyone ought to be invited to compose their own 'Thought for the Day' because of the way it forces one to think. Those reflections, therefore, are just that, my reflections on life as I see it happening around me. They carry no authority, they may well be heretical, they do not pretend to tell anyone else how to think; but if they goad or encourage anyone to do their own thinking about these things I shall be well content.

The reflections fall naturally into three sections, on the Personal, on Organizations and their workings, and on Society. The reflections reflect me. Inevitably. I have therefore added a 'personal preface' in which I try to reveal a little more of me and the way my beliefs about life and the meaning of life came to be shaped.

A Personal Preface

It started, I suppose, with the death of my father. So many things do start with a death. It makes one wonder whom and what one's own death will spring loose.

My father was a quiet man. He had been rector of the same country parish in Kildare in Southern Ireland for forty years when he retired, aged seventy-two. He was tired by then, understandably. For the last fourteen of those years he had also been Archdeacon of the Diocese. He died two years later.

I was in Paris at a business conference when I heard that he was dying. I flew back to Ireland, but he was unconscious by the time I got there and died the next day. His funeral, like all funerals in Ireland, was arranged for the day after tomorrow, a quiet family affair, back in the country church he had served for so long.

I was very fond of my father, but disappointed in him. He had turned down big city parishes, had settled for a humdrum life in the same little backwater. His life seemed to be a series of boring meetings and visits punctuated with the unchanging rhythm of Sundays, with old Mrs Atkinson and Eddie to lunch in the rectory afterwards. As a teenager I resolved never to go to church again, once I led my own life, and never to be poor again.

And so it was that, much to the amazement of my friends and family, I became an oil executive and was posted to the Far East to be in charge of Marketing in Sarawak – a job and a country both unknown in the rectory. I had a good time in Malaysia, mostly spending money and drinking too much beer. I came back fat and rather sleek, and also engaged, to a beautiful English girl whom I had met in Kuala Lumpur.

She didn't think much of an oil executive's life or of her predestined role as an oil executive's hostess, so I switched to the newly-discovered academic world of Business Studies, going to the United States to pick up another degree and coming back to the infant London Business School. Soon I was a professor, gallivanting around to conferences, consulting, lunching, dining, on the edge of the big time. A book had been published and articles galore. We had two young children, a flat in town and a cottage in the country. More than that, I was tremendously busy, with a diary crammed with engagements. Success!

It was with these thoughts in mind that I followed the hearse down the country roads to my father's funeral; a quiet end for a quiet man, I reflected. A pity that he never really understood what I was doing. When I became a professor I remember my mother's reaction to the news was to ask if this meant that I could now spend more time with the children.

Suddenly I noticed that we seemed to have a police escort; the local police had decided unasked to clear our route for the last few miles to the church. A nice compliment to a Protestant vicar in rural Catholic Ireland, but just as well because it was hard to thread our way between the queues of cars trying to get to the little country church. The place was packed, overflowing. How had they heard? He had only died the day before yesterday and there had just been the one notice in the paper.

The choir looked odd, too. Dressed in the little-boy surplices that I remembered from Sundays long ago but with older faces. I remembered some of them. Choir boys and choir girls reassembled from all the corners of Ireland, or from England too. They had dropped everything to be there. The Archbishop too, supposed to be in hospital, and still propped on a stick, was there to say to all of us how special my father had been and how he would be missed but remembered forever by so many whose lives he had touched.

As I stood by his grave, surrounded by people he had helped to marry and whose children he had later baptized and then seen marry in his church in their turn, as I saw the tears in the eyes of the hundreds of people who had come from everywhere to say farewell to this 'quiet' man, I turned away and began to think.

Who, I wondered, would come to my funeral with tears in their eyes? What is success and who was successful, me or my father? What is one's life for, and what is the point of our existence in this world? They are not exactly new questions. I had studied philosophy. I knew the theories. I had never applied them to myself before. Not seriously.

I went back to England. It was a long hot summer that year. I resolved to change my life and my priorities. I thought I might go to theological college, might become ordained, be a priest like my father. Luckily, I now think, the bishops whom I approached told me not to be so silly. If I wanted to serve God, as they put it, I could do it much better as a Professor of Business than in a dog-collar.

They encouraged me, actually, to apply for the post of Warden of St George's House in Windsor Castle. This is a small select study centre established by Prince Philip and the then Dean of Windsor, Robin Woods, to be a meeting place for people of influence in the churches and in other parts of society. It ran consultations on things like Justice, The Future of Work, Power and Responsibility in our Institutions, consultations at which captains of industry, trade union leaders, head teachers, civil servants and politicians mingled and debated with bishops and chaplains and each other. It was a place of retreat and reflection for busy people in a busy world, set in a courtyard behind St George's Chapel. It became my home and my obsession for the next four years.

From one extreme to another. I thought at first that they had left out a nought when I saw my salary. They provided me with a lovely house but the cost of carpeting it was more than my first year's pay. What was all this about never being poor again, I wondered. Life has a way of going full circle, and as for never going to church again, I lived in the shadow of the great Chapel of St George and attended with relish the early morning service there in the little upstairs chapel every day of every week. 'You've been to church three times today,' my startled mother-in-law said to my wife and myself once, 'and it's only Thursday!'

But I was also in charge of the study centre and was experiencing all the problems of moving into a new institution in a new field, a world where I was not known and where I knew not their ways. It was stressful. Before long I took myself off to a psychotherapist. 'What are you seeking to achieve?' he asked me. 'I just want to make the world, in some small way, a better place,' I replied. 'Oh, I see,' he said with heavy irony, 'so now we have the three of you, Jesus Christ, the Prophet Mohammed and Professor Charles Handy!' I blushed, rebuked and embarrassed, but I got the message: here I was sitting in his consulting room, sick at heart, and talking about changing the world. There was something somewhere about taking great beams out of one's own eyes first, I recalled. I needed to be surer about myself and my beliefs if I was going to be of any use to anyone else. To put it more crisply, being is essential to doing; who I am colours what I do. Was it not Dr Johnson who said, 'Who you are sounds so loudly in my ears that I can't hear what you say.'

He said something else, my psychotherapist. I had arrived late for one session. Hampstead is a long way from Windsor and the traffic can be bad. I got there at twenty minutes past the hour instead of on the hour. At 2.50 p.m. when I had been there thirty minutes his little alarm went 'ping', signalling that the normal fifty minute consultation was up. 'Oh dear,' I said, 'I've only just got going, have you anyone else coming?'

'No,' he said.

'Well, then, can I stay on?'

9

'No, I'm afraid not.'

'But I've only been here thirty minutes. I got delayed by the traffic.'

'That's your problem,' he said, 'not mine.'

I went away fuming, but then I reflected that he was right. I spent my life apologizing to people for things that were nothing to do with me, like the weather, the state of our street, or the rudeness of the local shopkeeper. If people arrived late for an appointment, *I* didn't cut short the appointment, I said, 'Oh bad luck, please don't concern yourself,' and would cheerfully change my plans for the day because of *their* poor scheduling, taking, as it were, their failings on my shoulders and feeling noble as I did it. This was, I now saw, to take responsibility away from them, to steal their choices. But was not this what Jesus Christ was supposed to have done, taken all our sins upon himself? No, I eventually decided, that had to be a misrepresentation of Christianity. It is not an escapist religion. We can't go off and do as we like and then dump all our sins or mistakes on the deity. That's garbage-can religion with God as the garbage can.

I was beginning to realize not only that theology was not as straightforward as it had seemed in the days of my youth but that it was also highly practical. I could not get on with my life or be at peace with myself until I had sorted out some of this stuff. Being and doing are inseparable.

Two months later I was invited by the Dean and Canons to preach the sermon at the Sunday morning service in St George's Chapel. It was, I was told, the first time that a layman had preached formally in that place since it was built in the sixteenth century. Be that as it may I was suitably overawed. I decided that it would be quite inappropriate for me to try to interpret the word of God so instead I set out to explain what I saw as the point and purpose of the study centre which sat at the end of the courtyard at the back of the Chapel. It was, I said, a place where we tried to connect people's beliefs with the problems of life and of work in today's world. If I am right, I said, the central message of Christianity is that religion is not about another life in another world but about our life in this world – God became Man, as the Bible puts it. The search for that connection between belief and action is never-ending and always changing because the world and its problems are always changing. The beliefs may remain the same but their applications will always need to be rethought by each of us each year, even each day. We are forever going to be searchers after truth.

I need not have worried too much about my sermon. I had forgotten about the verger. The verger, who is the master of ceremonies on these occasions, had never been too keen on the idea. 'Sit where you like,' he had said when I asked him about the protocol, 'and wear what you like. This has never happened before. There is no precedent.' I got the distinct impression that he hoped it would never happen again. I should not therefore have been terribly surprised when the microphones failed just after I got up to speak and did not function again that morning. The ears of the faithful were not afflicted by any possible heresies that day and I learnt, yet again, that those who control the technology will always wield great negative power, so that it is as well to have them on your side. I was pleased when the verger came up to me the next day to apologize for a 'malfunctioning of the audio system' and also to ask for a copy of my address. 'Those who heard it said that it made a lot of sense.' But that, of course, was afterwards.

The ears of the faithful may not have been harmed but I learnt a lot. It was an Irishman who said, 'How do I know what I think until I hear what I say?' and I am an Irishman. It remains the best clue to learning that I know of. The need to communicate forces you to work out what you want to say and, after that, it doesn't matter too much if anyone listens or not, because what they ought to do is to work out in their turn what they want to say. Preaching, you might say, gets in the way of learning, except for the preacher.

Over four years I listened to some six thousand people in small seminars and consultations find out what they thought when they heard what they said. Some of what they said was inspiring, some was boring, some bizarre. You couldn't always predict which mouths would say which. Two years after I left the place a businessman asked me to lunch, to thank me he said. 'What for?' I asked, over the drinks. 'Because of that weekend in Windsor some years back. I heard myself saying that the sense of responsibility that goes with ownership is so important that it shouldn't be a minority right. I went away and thought about that and decided to share the ownership of my business with my workers. The agreement was signed yesterday, hence this lunch.'

Is this anything to do with religion – I used to ask myself – with the hymns and the psalms which the choir sing so beautifully in that Chapel? I'm sure it is. I'm sure that our beliefs should, and do, infect our lives. If we try to live our lives in separate compartments, one for doing, perhaps, and one for being, why then for part of the time we are living a lie, 'the truth is not in us'. That I found and still find, is not very comfortable.

Since the day of that sermon I have been trying to bring my being and my doing closer together. In time I left Windsor. It was time to go, anyway, but I was growing increasingly uncomfortable with the need to fit into my role. It is hard for being and doing to weld into one when for part of your doing you have to act a part which is not totally 'you'. All of us, in organizations, are 'role occupants' and very few of us could claim that there is a perfect match between us and our role. That, I think, is part of the problem with organizations and part of their seduction. They force us, or allow us, depending on your viewpoint, to escape from ourselves and to play a part. It can be fun, for a while. It can be damaging in the end.

To me the only answer, I gradually realized, was to be my own master and employer. Today I am a self-employed writer and teacher. It is financially more perilous but in every other way more secure. I can't now escape from myself in my work, but these days I don't want to so much. Being and doing are closer.

It is no part of my mission to foist my beliefs on to other people. That would run counter to my philosophy of life and learning. We each have to do the searching for ourselves. Nevertheless, some clues to my beliefs are there in these reflections. My concern is only to point to what *I* see as the meaning in things and to the ultimate purpose in life in order to encourage other people to find their meaning and their purpose. The nicest comments I ever had on those broadcasts were from the man who said, 'You set me thinking for the whole of that day,' and from the woman who wrote, 'I had been bedridden for three years bemoaning my bad luck in losing both my legs. After listening, I decided that I had to do something with my life so I got up and enrolled in the local college.'

PERSONAL

Waiting for the Mountain to Move

When I get depressed I try to think of Eric Fletcher. Eric Fletcher was a Teesider who, famously, thrust his thousand job-rejection letters under Mrs Thatcher's nose on her tour of his region and stole all her glory from her for a day. Two weeks later he got a placement with a job-training scheme, learning to be a printer, armed, moreover, with an interview report which describes him as bright, capable and articulate.

Mind you, I always thought that he was underselling himself when he described himself as 'just a labouring man', incapable of learning a new skill. Anyone who has the stamina to apply for a thousand jobs and the gumption to present them to a Prime Minister has to have *something* going for him.

I hope it works out for him, because it might mean not just a change in his living standards but in the whole way he looks at life. It was, I think, the sense of helplessness which he projected, and which had, apparently, infected his whole family, which made so many identify with him but exasperated so many others.

17

But I have, myself, had a glimpse of how he must have felt. My blackest times are those when I feel that my life is out of my control. Things are happening, or not happening, and I seem powerless to stop them or change them. It then gets even worse when I start to hope, yes and sometimes pray, that some outside being will intervene to put things right and *still* nothing happens.

It reminds me of Kierkegaard's story of the traveller in the hill country who came to a village only to find his road onward blocked by a mountain. So he sat and waited for the mountain to move. Years later he was still there, old now and white-haired, still waiting. Then he died, but he was long remembered in the village as a proverb, 'the man who waited for the mountain to move'.

Kierkegaard's point is that God doesn't move mountains (nor send stock markets crashing); *we climb* mountains with God's help. Don't therefore look for Him, or His agent, outside. Look for Him inside, in *you*, and using His eyes find *new* bits of you which you never knew were there.

I go along with the fourteenth-century author of that great mystical work *The Cloud of Unknowing*, 'Swink and sweat in all that thou canst and mayest,' he says, 'for to get thee a true knowing and feeling of thyself as thou art. And then, I trow, soon after that thou wilt get thee a true knowing and feeling of God as He is.' There is, you see, more to all of us than we think there is. We *must* believe that. Swink and sweat to find yourself. It has to be worth it.

Buffalo Bill or Me?

What's in a name? Quite a lot, seemingly. At any rate lots of us are at it, changing names that is. Companies do it, sometimes with bewildering rapidity – designing company logos is the new growth industry. Whole countries do it. People do it, particularly when they marry or unmarry. I dropped the name Charlie when I went to college and became Charles – a sign of my accelerating pomposity, my parents said then.

Changing one's name is, it seems, a self-awarded licence to be different. In fact it is interesting to note that many people these days do *not* change their names when they marry – a signal perhaps that they do *not* intend to be different. And I remember long ago going to a rather trendy workshop in America where you were invited to invent a new name before you came with a promise that no one, not even the seminar leader, would know your real one. There were two Buffalo Bills, I recall, in that group, one Marilyn Monroe and one Anon. After much agony I went as myself, ashamed at first of my lack of imagination, then proud of my integrity. What it meant however, the seminar leader told me, was that I was there under false pretences – I didn't want to find a new 'me'.

A new name however is only the start of it. The name signals a determination to be different, to have a new beginning, a rebirth even, but who then will we decide to be? Oneself, I hope. I used to tell my students not to look over their shoulders, meaning that they did not need to ape their colleagues, that they should set their *own* standards and make their *own* definitions of success.

Bishop Richard Harries, in one of his books, has a nice story about a rabbi with an unpronounceable name, Zuzya of Hannipol. ' " In the coming world," said the Rabbi, "they will not ask me why were you not Moses but why were you not Zuzya?" ' and as for me, I don't want to die knowing that I had only pretended to live.

So how do I know when I'm me? It's a good question for all of us – individuals, companies, political parties even. It's like beauty, I think, or being in tune. You can't define it, but you know when it's there and when it's not there. You have to trust your eye or your ear and you have, above all, to believe that there is a tune for *you*, or as St Paul put it to the cosmopolitan and fun-loving Corinthians, the yuppies of yesteryear, you must believe that the Spirit is in each and every one of us, with a different message for each but for the good of all. If you don't believe that you'll just be a sounding brass or a clashing cymbal, or today a portable fax and a personal phone.

Life is not a Dress Rehearsal

Were you around at the time of the Live-Aid concert in aid of the Ethiopian famine victims? Perhaps you were there. By all accounts more people listened around the world than ever listened to a pop concert before and gave more money. I'm only now getting my mind around all the noughts. The mere thought of organizing such an extravaganza, awash with egos and technology, still leaves me gasping, and I loved at the time the sight on my TV of so many people having fun while doing good. I grew up thinking that doing good meant dark clothes and serious faces. But I think that what impressed me most of all was that Bob Geldof had had a dream, a great huge colossal dream, and decided to do something about it. I dream of great ideas too, sometimes, though not quite as great as that, but then I think that if it was all *that* great someone would have done it already; or anyway it will be easier to do next year when I've more time, or when the children have left home, or when . . . or when . . . But he damn well went and did it!!

I remembered then my friend who suddenly announced the other day, apropos of nothing in particular, that she, at forty-five, had suddenly realized that life was not a dress rehearsal. Yet there I was, at fifty-two, still wondering what I was going to be when I grew up. It's a nice thought that old age is always ten years older than you are now, but it can lead to postponing the future till you end up as the man with a bright future behind him! What ever happened to old so-and-so?

We all know people who live lives of deferred gratification, waiting till they're fifty, or retired, or just a bit richer, to live where they want to live, do what they want to do, go where they want to go. How many of them ever get to do it? And how many of them, when they get there, still find it worth all the waiting and the striving and the saving?

Life isn't a dress rehearsal. The party's for real. Perhaps that is what is meant by Christianity's insistence that God became Man. Religion, God, heaven were not separated out but all mixed in with us on earth. Life wasn't an ante-room for heaven but the stage for heaven, should we choose to play on it.

Quite transforming it was for me, that thought. Stop compiling a curriculum vitae, it said to me, a list of jobs and roles, an obituary notice to show St Peter; get on with living as if you were already in heaven. And heaven, for me, isn't harps and angels and fluffy clouds, but joy and love and laughter and, most of all, a sense of timeless being, at peace with myself and my God. You see it, don't you, in the faces of those about to die, or hear it in the words of my not-so-old friend recently, given six months to live, who said he felt a much nicer person suddenly, all hassle over, all enmities forgiven. But why wait for death to taste of heaven?

So, *carpe diem*, as the Romans put it. Postpone your dreams no longer. One man *can* move mountains, or at least fill Wembley Stadium. Being good can indeed be fun. *This* play's for real, I reckon, so today, I say to myself, why not *be* what you want to become.

Image Enhancement

I was sitting one day in a tiny windowless room watching them edit a television documentary. 'Wipe the traffic noise, Tim,' the editor said. 'Right,' he said, 'no – now it's a bit empty – what about some birdsong?' They went to the bookcase and took out a tape labelled 'Birdsong'. Suddenly the scene on the documentary came alive, with birdsong now, not traffic. 'Hey, you can't do that,' I exclaimed. 'Why ever not?' They looked round at me, the naïve outsider. 'Well,' I said, 'because it's not true, there weren't any birds there; it's a lie!' 'Nonsense,' they said, 'it's just *image enhancement*, you wouldn't want us to film you with no clothes on, would you, so you dress up to look nice.' Image enhancement, we're all at it all the time!

I suppose we are. I don't want the estate agent to tell prospective purchasers about the noise from the endless parties in the flat above, so I suggest that 'convivial' might cover it, if anyone asks. I even saw one house described as having central heating 'sensibly confined to the ground floor'! I preen myself in front of the mirror to make sure that I look a touch slimmer and younger than I really am – just a little lie.

Most people would feel a bit of image enhancement does no one any harm. There are even courses on it if you feel the need. But at some stage image enhancement becomes a downright lie. How does one know where to draw that line? I don't know any general answer to that. What I do know, however, is that living a lie is very uncomfortable – unless of course your whole life is one big act, and I know a few people like that too! If we deceive *ourselves*, you might say, the truth is not in us. These words are actually a slight misquotation from St John's Gospel. St John really says, 'If we say we have no sin, we deceive ourselves and the truth is not in us.' In other words, no one expects anyone to be perfect; indeed we often like and respect people even more if we know their little frailties. Image enhancement can be counter-productive if it makes you, or it, seem too good to be true.

We should not, I think, be so afraid of ourselves. For many a year I tried to be something I wasn't with some fairly strenuous image enhancement. But the nice thing about growing older is that you eventually stop pretending. Then it is that you discover that being oneself, being truly oneself, is really rather fun. You can say what you like, see whom you like, tell it like it really is. What's more, it turns out that no one was taken in by the image anyway. These days I can vouch for it, 'The truth will set you free.'

The San Francisco Earthquake

I had things I wanted to share with you this morning. Suddenly they seemed rather beside the point. I was speaking with a friend in San Francisco only last night, at one o'clock in their afternoon, because I am going there next month. 'It will be lovely,' he said. 'We'll go up to the wine country, the leaves will be turning.' Right now my *heart* is turning. John, over there, and Pat, I hope you are all right, I hope you weren't travelling on the Bay Bridge at five o'clock. To all those who were, to all those anywhere else in that beautiful city who may have been hurt, who may have had loved ones lost or hurt, my heart goes out.

What does one say at times like this? Such times have happened before, they will happen again. Everybody has always known about the San Andreas fault, everyone knew that it would happen some day, but not, we always hoped and prayed, not this day, not this day.

I will go out now and try to ring my friends, we will all do that if we know people there. It's at times like this that you need friends. There isn't often much that we can do, but at least we are there. It is, I think, a great mistake to be frightfully English and polite and leave people alone with their grief – they just feel left, they miss the politeness.

As for me, I shall remember that this night *my* soul *too* might be required of me. All sorts of things suddenly now seem insignificant. Why on earth, I wonder now, was I worried about that insurance claim? Why was I so upset by that little argument in the office?

The trouble is, having had my priorities readjusted by something like this, or by some personal brush with death, I so quickly lose those new perspectives when life resumes. This time, I tell myself, I will not postpone any more my big resolutions for life.

I have spent my life wondering what I was going to do when I grew up. I still do it now, in my mid-fifties. Well, heaven, as I understand it, is *not* some distant Nirvana. Heaven, or the potential of it, is all around us. I shall go out today and try to live as if I was fit for it. I must go now and ring my friends.

NOTE

I was woken at 6.0 a.m. on 18th October 1989 to be told that there had been a major earthquake in San Francisco during the night (their late afternoon). No one yet knew how bad. This piece was broadcast at 7.45 a.m. We met John and Pat a month later. They were OK but still shocked by what had happened to many of their friends and family. We went up to the wine country.

The White Stone

American Presidential elections are strange affairs, I say to myself every four years, and remarkably long and boring affairs too. I suppose the rationale is that if you can endure a two-year-long election you can endure anything.

The curious thing about the whole of the process is the pretence that one of these two men will run the country, alone. No one runs big organizations on their own these days, let alone countries. It has to be a team affair, although of course the man, or woman, at the head has an enormous influence. One would like therefore to know how good these two people are at running teams and more important still, at picking them. It might even be sensible to elect the team and not just the leader.

Picking teams is not easy. If they are all clones or toadies of the leader they won't work. Nor will they work well if everyone is the same sort of person as everyone else. They once staged a competition in the Albert Hall between a team of company chairmen, a team of trade union leaders and a team of students. They asked them each to build a tower with Lego bricks. The chairmen came last. They all of them wanted to talk strategy which was what they were good at, not to do the actual building.

Teams need people of all sorts of types and talents. In the jargon of my world we call them shapers, finishers and evaluators and such like. St Paul, I'm glad to say, uses a richer language when he writes to the Corinthians, talking of the different gifts of the Spirit, and the need for each part of the body to make its own contribution. The point is the same, however; you need mixes of all sorts to make things work.

This may be a problem for the leader, who has to choose the team, but it's good news for the rest of us. Lots of mixes of talents and types mean lots of room for all our individual differences. To put it bluntly, there is bound to be a team out there somewhere, sometime, where our particular personality and our particular talent would help. Some find it early, some find it late, and if *you* haven't found team or talent yet, then persevere.

When I doubt that myself, like every Monday morning, I get strange comfort from a peculiar verse in the Book of Revelation. 'To anyone who prevails, the Spirit says, I will give a white stone, on which is written a new name which no one knows except he who receives it.' It is that white stone which will tell me, I believe, who I really am and what I'm really for. When I will get it I know not. That I *will* get it I am sure.

Sticking-Points

I'm lucky, I suppose. I've never really been pushed up against death. I don't know how I would behave in a hijack – I'm rather afraid that the answer might be 'shamingly'. Lucky? Well, on second thoughts, perhaps not so lucky because I've never had to work out what my sticking-points are.

Sticking-points. The Bishop used the word when he was with me and a group of managers some years back. 'What's your sticking-point?' he asked them. 'What would you not do, no matter what?' 'Murder,' they said, 'or steal or lie.' Yet, on reflection, they weren't so sure. Would you not lie to save your life on that hijacked plane – if you thought it would work? Would you lie, or at least conceal the truth, to do a better deal in business? To sell your house or trade in your car?

The Bishop's point, I think, was that all life is based on some assumption of principle. There can never be enough laws and rules and inspectors to cover everything, particularly in organizations and in business –

even in families. Life would get too complicated – and too expensive.

I remember taking a group of clergy some years back to see around the Lloyds insurance building and to meet some of the agents, underwriters and brokers, and finally the Chairman himself. 'Very impressive it is,' said the clergy, 'it all seems very efficient but it must be tremendously testing morally.' The Chairman looked bemused, I remember. 'Why?' he asked. 'Well,' they said, 'everyone seems to have two or more roles, two or more conflicting loyalties, there aren't many rules or inspectors so you have to trust people to act on principle, honourably.' 'Of course,' he said. Alas, not long after events were to prove that unprincipled people can thrive in a system based mainly on principle.

It was ironic, I reflected then, that just as Lloyds had begun to make more rules and to put up some barriers between its conflicting loyalties the stock market started to dismantle its barriers in order to remain competitive. Nobody realized at the time that the so-called Big Bang was going to make Principle and People of Principle even more precious in the City.

And not just in the City. If organizations of any sort are to be left reasonably unfettered, if individuals are to be free to exercise their own initiative, then one's personal principles and values cannot be left on the coat-stand when you walk through the office door. Principles don't belong in one box, work in another, even if it would be convenient for some of us to think that they do.

Indeed, I do know some people who seem to operate with two sets of principles – one Sunday-best for home consumption, another more, shall we say, pragmatic for downtown. They call it sensible. I call it moral schizo-phrenia and a recipe for breakdown both of the individual and the organization.

I don't think it's an accident that, on the whole, the most efficient organizations are the most principled ones. Trust, after all, costs much less than checking, but for trust to work you need to have principles, and sticking-points – and they only come, I believe, from a set of beliefs.

Trust and the Plumber

Compared with all the dramas being acted out on the news these days my problems with my plumber may sound trivial. But they too may be clues to the world we live in, a barometer on the weather ahead. He's a nice chap, our plumber, and I trust him, so when I asked him to fit an outside tap on the garden wall and agreed a price I thought that that was that.

He fixed the tap all right, but instead of putting it above the gulley so that any drips would drain away he had put it three feet to the left where it would slop all over the grass. I could see why, it was easier for him to put it there and he was always one for the short cut. When I complained he said 'Oh – it's against Water Board regulations to put a tap above a drain. Contamination you see.' It sounded a bit odd but, as I said, he's a nice chap and I trusted him.

'Don't be silly,' said my wife, 'he's having you on.' She rang the Water Board and of course he *was* talking nonsense, telling lies to get himself out of a corner.

Well, I forgave him because I wanted him to sort it out; and he did, reluctantly. But I seem to have been required to forgive an awful lot of people lately for broken promises, missed deadlines, bad work or lost money; people I trusted but who let me down.

Can it be, I wondered, as I sat, like Job, on the building site that should have been my home, that I am really expected to take books like the Bible seriously when it says that I should forgive my brother seventy times seven when he let me down every single time? The answer, I'm afraid, is 'yes' if I want him to continue to be my brother. That's not piety, that's practicality, because no relationship can survive and grow unless we are prepared to trust and to forgive when the trust goes wrong, again and again and again. No forgiveness means no relationship.

That's the bad weather which I feel coming in our society today. Trust and forgiveness are not much in evidence today because too often neither party cares whether the relationship continues or not, neither supplier nor customer, neither organization nor contractor, sometimes neither husband nor wife. Enterprise can then come to mean 'getting away with it'; prudent people will 'trust but verify', as President Reagan used to say, while careful people watch their backs and call their lawyers.

It's a sad world, I think, when we can genuinely pray 'forgive us for *not* forgiving those who sin against us'. It's a sign that trust and love and friendship have failed, have become the luxuries of life but not its basics. For myself, I will try to choose my plumbers better and *then* will persevere, trusting against the odds, forgiving if I can because, in the end, relationships matter more than perfect plumbing, and trust is cheaper than lawyers.

NOTE

Much to my surprise, my plumber was listening when this piece was broadcast. I was worried. I need not have been. He was tickled pink, as they say, to be on the air and promised to be totally trustworthy in future. Where there is trust there is hope!

Rat Races and Whirlpools

The flame will be extinguished in the Olympic stadium on Sunday. Perhaps it might be better to quench it today say some. What price now the proud claim that it is the taking part that matters, not the winning?

I am sure that most of the nine thousand three hundred athletes out there are sickened and saddened by what is happening. This was not the world they dreamt of when first they discovered that they were fleet of foot and strong of arm. They went out for a swim, as it were, and found a rat race.

As has happened before, the brief fortnight of the Olympics is spelling out a central message of our times. Not this year the posturing of great powers or the anger of the Third World but instead the terrible pressures and dilemmas of a world where to succeed can mean fame and fortune almost beyond count and to fail is to drop right out. And it is going on everywhere, not just in sport.

I watch some of my students at the business school

take on jobs which will, they know, require 100-hour weeks, all year, each year, cramming what used to be a forty-five year working life into twenty or twenty-five pressurized years, and then what I wonder? I see others postponing motherhood until it is too late and I have watched my son and his friends, these last three months, shut themselves up in a dark studio every day and every night until 4.00 a.m. to make their album. He is only twenty. There is more to life than just this music, I say. There is for instance, the sunlight which you never see. He answers in the catchphrase of our day, 'there is no alternative' if he wants to succeed.

I admire the dedication. I worry that they lose their balance, their way and their sense of truth. What makes young bankers, I wonder, risk their careers for £3,000 profit on an insider deal when they know, they must know, that finance houses have their own sort of drug test?

Caught up each in our own whirlpool, what the *others* do, quickly becomes the measure of what *we* should do, of what is right. In my world we call it 'group think'. 'You people,' the Indian mystic said to me, 'have lost yourselves in *busyness*.' I could be more dramatic and say that we are in danger of giving away our souls.

To refind those souls we must learn to leave our whirlpools from time to time, to withdraw and then re-enter, refreshed and redirected. We need, I feel, to walk awhile in other people's worlds, or, like the desert fathers of old, to go out at times into the desert and vomit up our double, the one that isn't us. We need, or least I need, a regular place of stillness to reconnect myself with the God I believe is in me, my true me.

'Be still then, and know that I am God,' sang the psalmist, but it's hard today to hear his song amid the din of all our doings.

NOTE

The Seoul Olympic Games finished on Sunday 2nd October 1988. They were marred by several disqualifications for drug-taking.

Beyond the Market

In 1938, when Chamberlain returned from Munich with his little piece of paper, T. S. Eliot wondered whether Britain was now anything more than a collection of banks and a decent interest rate. Given the attention we pay in the media to the questions of the financial world he might wonder today whether we were anything more than a rather dishevelled stock market and a slightly *indecent* interest rate.

Coming from a Business School, as I do, I am well aware of the necessity for markets of all sorts, be they for fruit and cheese in an Italian village or for stocks and shares in an electronic one. They are simply the best way that anyone has yet found of putting an acceptable price on things. But we should be careful not to push a good idea to unhealthy extremes or we may be ham-strung by our own invention. Money, after all, was made for man's convenience, not the other way round.

To tell you the truth, I find *all* the markets rather depressing these days. Like many others, I suspect. My little portfolio of shares is presumably even littler today. I don't think that there *is* a market for my house and I don't dare to find out. My pension, I suspect, is not now all it promised to be and the market for middle-aged university teachers is decidedly bleak. My net worth, as they say, is clearly on a downturn.

My net worth but not, thank God, my real worth. I mean 'thank God' quite literally because I believe that it must ultimately be by His doing that I still *know*, in my heart, that I do have real value, no matter what the markets say. When the world depresses, that thought keeps me sane. I also cannot help but notice that the old cliché really is true, the important things in life *are* free, they are outside *any* market.

The birds were singing this morning, I noticed with relief. I didn't, couldn't buy that. Nor can you or I buy friendship or the respect of friends. Or the look in the eyes of your children. My twenty-three-year-old daughter astonished her grandmother the other day by saying that her parents were parents no longer, but her very good friends. Her grandmother snorted in disbelief but we were tickled pink. To us that is being valued and that's beyond price.

I know, too, from bitter experience, that you can't buy a clear conscience. I still have bad dreams over something I did to someone thirty years ago. No money will rid me of that memory. Only his forgiveness. I could go on. You can't buy, I hope, the love of the one by your side, nor truth, nor sincerity, nor faithfulness. That cannot be by chance. God, it is clear, does not need markets to tell Him what things are worth. Nor should we. Not for the things that *really* matter.

SPG

Every year, it seems, the big banks decide to write off tens and hundreds of millions of pounds as provision against bad debtors; sometimes it is because some Third World countries have not repaid their loans but some-times, recently, it has been because some big businesses which they helped to finance have regrettably collapsed. Just occasionally I wonder why it is that when the banks do this they are commended for their prudence, but if ever I, in my small way, were to make such gross errors of judgement it would be called an unforgivable mistake. It's wonderful what you can do with words.

Words and money mattered too in the Irish rectory where I grew up. Each week my parents would prepare and exchange their personal accounts, in an attempt to keep some track of their spending. It was a weekly agony for my mother who could never remember what she had spent on what. I used to try to help. 'Why,' I once asked, 'do you spend so much sometimes on the SPG when we are so poor?' A child of the rectory, I knew about the

SPG; it was the Society for the Propagation of the Gospel in Foreign Parts, a famous missionary society. 'Hush,' said my mother, 'and never tell your father, but SPG really stands for Something, Probably Grub.'

It was my first realization that accountancy can sometimes be more of a creative art than a science. Looking back now I think that my father always knew and she knew that he knew but they both realized that 'keeping count' was a valuable discipline, even allowing for the SPG.

Digging deeper, I came to realize that it is part of the tradition of every religion that we should have to render an account of our life at the end of that life. It would be prudent, therefore, that we should prepare for ourselves, from time to time, some interim accounts, some trial balances, showing what we have taken from life so far and what we have put back into it.

Balance sheets should balance. There should be as much on the giving side as on the getting side; and balance sheets should grow. Empty and emptying people haven't much to give. Of course, I am not talking money now. Other things are rather more important, when it comes to measuring one's *spiritual* net worth. To each of us, there are some special assets given, to be used not wasted. Perhaps it is time for an audit.

The difference is that if, by laziness, or error, our spiritual net worth declines in one accounting period, then, lucky us, we are not written off, there is no heavenly receivership, just the expectation that things will be noticeably better in the period ahead. I am forgiven but not released. That's tough spiritual banking, but, I think, good banking.

The Autumn Cull

I discovered last week what they mean when they say that chestnut trees are self-pruning. They mean that huge branches fall off in the wind, mainly on top of my car!

All in all it has been quite a week for pruning – if you can call it that; decimation might be a better word; trees and share prices toppling wherever you look. The autumn cull you might say. I have even heard some people talk of it as God's own cull – His reminder to the South-East of England and to the City that riches guarantee nothing in this world.

Well, useful reminder it may be, but I don't myself believe in that kind of magician in the sky, doing what my insurance company used to call His Acts of God.

But I do believe in pruning. I notice that after its rather dramatic bit of self-pruning my chestnut tree is still standing. Cut back to its essentials, it survived, while others all around it tumbled.

It's an old old message. Cut back to your essentials and

43

you'll be stronger, better able not only to survive the odd storm but freer to take on new challenges. It applies to people just as much as it does to trees and to share portfolios and to every organization everywhere.

Get rid of the clutter of your riches, Jesus told the young man, then you can be of some use to me. Be like the lilies, He said on another occasion, uncluttered they don't worry about the future, *and* He practised what He preached.

But it's easier said than done, I find. Myself, I *like* a lot of clutter. It keeps me busy. If I'm totally honest I often want to lose myself in busyness and I suspect that quite a lot of people are the same. I guess some would say that we are lucky to have the opportunity.

Yet looking out now at my chestnut tree, stripped down to its stem, I realize why it is that people often come out of a severe illness with a much clearer perspective on life, dismissing now as unimportant all the little nigs and nags, unconcerned about belongings and possessions, living each day to the hilt, serenely impervious to the worries of tomorrow. They have been forcibly self-pruned and I know I envy them.

The dramatic events of these few days have made me realize that it is silly to wait for the blows of nature to recall us to our essentials – silly and a bit risky. Better surely to take it in hand ourselves.

At one level that means getting one's priorities straight, giving time to the things that will endure, like our loved ones, long after bank statements and job titles have gone on their way to the bin, but at a deeper, much deeper, level. I am talking about a journey in search of one's soul. About that I know only this, that it is a dark and lonely journey but probably, in the end, the only one which we all should start on before the next autumn storm.

NOTE

On the night of Friday 16th October 1987 the fiercest gale of the century swept across southern Britain, decimating its woodlands. Monday 19th October was Black Monday when share markets crashed all round the world.

Marathons not Horse Races

The season of Lent should be a reminder to us to find more space for contemplation and rebalancing in our busy lives. 'Not so,' said one lady. She thought that the point of Lent was self-denial. 'Self-denial,' I said to her, 'has been the bane of this society and of its religions.'

No, I am not advocating some kind of orgy of self-indulgence, and yes, I do believe that self-control is important. What worries me is the whole set of attitudes which implies that being pleased with yourself is somehow suspect, that being different is dangerous, that cold showers are good for you, that high standards mean lots of losers, and that putting people down is the best way to make them spring up.

To put it bluntly, if we really did love our neighbours as ourselves most of our neighbours would have a pretty raw deal. Or, to put it another way, too much of our society seems to be designed to make most of us feel like losers most of the time, be it our examination system, our class system or our organizations. It's as if we were governed by the philosophy of the horse race in which only the first three count and the rest are also-rans.

You know, it's just possible that the mass marathon will come to be seen as the most important social invention of our age. In those marathons, you will have noticed, everyone who finishes gets a medal and winning means beating your own target, not the other runners. Why couldn't everything be like that? In some Japanese schools every child gets a prize, for *something*, and in the best of American firms you get awards for *trying*, not just for winning.

Does it matter? You bet it does, and I'll tell you why. When winning is so important, but so difficult, the best strategy must be to at least avoid losing. So, lower your sights, keep your head down and above all, don't try too hard. That way, if you fail you can always blame your laziness not your lack of ability and you can explain the laziness by claiming that the game wasn't worth the candle. I'm afraid that where humility is the mode, then apathy is the mood!

It's crazy, isn't it? I mean I need to be stroked, psychologically and positively, by someone for something *every day*. If I'm not, I get depressed and my energy slumps. And if me, then maybe others too. No wonder we the British do so pitifully in the economic effort stakes.

It's not only crazy, it's wrong. We are each meant to be different, aren't we? We are each given a bundle of talents, as I see it, in trust, to be used to improve our bit of creation and the lot of others. To ignore these talents in ourselves, to deny ourselves, is to spit in the face of the creator. To suppress them in others is tyranny.

Charles Handy

So, why not love yourselves a little today and then love others. It's not soft! And if you ever want a thought for Lent – don't give something up, take something on.

The Pendulum Principle

For four years I lived in the shadows of one of England's loveliest churches, the Chapel of St George in Windsor Castle, built in the same style as King's College Chapel in Cambridge and in the same period.

There were services there every morning and every evening and five of them on Sunday. I went to at least one and usually two every day, except, interestingly, on Sundays. What had happened, I wondered, to my adolescent determination never to go to church again?

I went because I wanted to, needed to, not at all because I had to. I had in my own experience stumbled across what Bruce Reed once called the oscillation theory of the Church. We live, as it were, on a pendulum swinging back and forth between activity and recreation. We need both. The pendulum must swing or the clock runs down.

Recreation however can be more than rest. Separate the word out into re-creation and it takes on a more powerful meaning, a sense of recharging combined with a touch of rebirth or newness. We should come out of the process not only refreshed but a little different.

We each need our stability zones to escape to in the hurly-burly of life. For some it may be the golf-course, for some, paradoxically, the routine of the commuter train, for others the garden or the pub. For me, for those four years, it was the Chapel of St George, but it was, I found, a stability zone with shove!

The form of service, I discovered, had its own momentum. The words are designed to draw you in, pour balm and forgiveness over you, and then push you out into the world to 'live and to work' to the glory of God. And it worked; I went in tired or depressed and would come out with new determination and a new spring in my step.

And that was in spite of not being allowed to join in the singing, which was, I used to think, the point of going to church. In the Chapel the choir did it for you, and quite beautifully. That released me, I found, to lose myself in the music, in the beauty of the building, in the mystery of life. 'Being' there was as important as 'doing' in that act of worship. God, as so many have discovered, is in the stillness of things.

I needed this re-creation every day, but never on Sundays because Sundays contained no work. For some the Sunday or the Sabbath recharging can last the week. Some may make do with a monthly shot. I needed it daily and I wish now that I still had that chapel outside my door every morning and every evening. Chapels, however, are a luxury, and even, perhaps, an unnecessary artefact. We ought to be able to use just the beauty of the morning, the quiet of the evening, the touch of friends or the peace of silence to pull back, draw breath, take strength and push out again.

It is the pendulum which makes the clock go round so the pendulum must not get stuck, at one end or the other. It is as easy to lose oneself in the busyness of the church and of its service as it is in the busyness of life. So 'Swing, my people, Swing,' as the singer said.

ORGANIZATIONS

Last Month We Closed a Factory

Last month we closed a factory.

When I say 'we' I mean the small business of which I am a part-time Director.

I don't suppose that these decisions are ever taken lightly, and this one certainly wasn't. But we had to face the facts: the factory had been losing money for two years and we could not let it bleed the rest of the business to death.

The business logic was clear. The human logic was just awful. How do you explain to people who have been working harder than ever, and producing more than ever before, that it was all useless – the stuff still sold at a loss, the more they made the more we lost. Economics can be a baffling science.

We listened to men, and women, telling us what it would be like to lose their jobs in an area where there were no new jobs. Many would never have a paid job again and it wouldn't be their fault. I felt like a judge passing sentence on the innocent.

Whose fault *was* it? Some said it was ours for not keeping them in jobs until all the money ran out, just in case things turned up. But we saw, all too clearly, that if we didn't close that factory now the whole lot would go. Isn't it better that some should go so that others might live? Not if it's you that goes, it isn't. It may be glorious to die for one's country but it isn't yet glorious to be made redundant for your firm. Should it be?

Some knew it was no one's fault. Nothing lasts for ever. New technology, or new habits, put paid to many things we took for granted. The candles I went to bed with every night when I was a boy in the depths of the country are now, for us, kept for special occasions. The electric light is easier for us but it was tough on the candlemakers. Death and then new life, in business as in nature. It's OK if it's nature and winter is followed by spring but it's tougher in business when only winter is on offer, and spring is in other parts of the country and for other skills.

'Get on your bike then,' the man said, but did he know that only ten per cent of the unemployed have bikes?

Some blamed the system. 'If it all belonged to everyone then everyone could have jobs,' they said. Not in that plant they couldn't, and not at those wages. You can change the owners but that doesn't change the cost of the product.

Some accused us of playing God. We were, they thought, sitting in that peculiar kind of heaven called a Board Room disposing of people's lives to suit our own grand design. Playing God? It didn't feel like that at all, unfortunately, at least not my kind of god.

My god would have found a way to give *each individual* the glimpse of new life in this kind of death and the means to grasp that life. My god would have found some light to shine on each person's darkness, some way of giving new meaning to each life, some way of discovering new talents in each of them and pushing them towards new opportunities. My god would have made them feel sure that they lived on, even when the factory died.

We did our best to do all this but I'm afraid it won't be enough for many at that plant, and many won't even believe we meant it. After all, institutions, no matter how well-intentioned, no matter who owns them or runs them, are no match for God. Perhaps no one should expect them to be.

Quality

I need to tell you about Richard, my friend. Richard was recently made head of a decent-sized business. 'One of the first things I did,' he told me, 'was to gather all the workforce together. I told them that I was not going to stand for second-class work going out, we had to produce quality, to be the best. I expected grumbles but instead they almost started to cheer.' 'You can't imagine,' they told him, 'how ashamed we have been in the past of some of the stuff we have sent out of these doors, but we were always told that we could not afford to do it better.' 'I'm telling you,' he said to them, 'that we can't afford *not* to do it better.' 'OK,' they said, 'but you'll have to get better presses than this one, can't do top quality work on inferior machines.' 'Point taken,' he said, 'but give me time. It will take time.'

I found it a heart-warming story, because I have always believed that no one in their heart of hearts *really* wants to do shoddy work.

But of course quality does take time to work, time for

the customers to come back again, time for the word to spread. And it takes courage: courage to sit out that first dip in profits, courage to hold the investors at bay, courage to outface the doubters and the faint of heart.

Still, this isn't meant to be a lecture on good business practice. I told the story because it seems to me to get to the heart of the human condition.

Quality, doing what you know is the best, what is the truth, will always work in the end, *if* you stick with it and if you will give it time. The second-best always turns out to be unsatisfying and, ultimately, unsustainable. 'I passed? didn't I,' I said, crossly, to my Headmaster once. 'You passed, yes,' he said, 'but it wasn't your best and you'll regret it.' Silly old fool, I said at the time. Now I know better.

The great religions, at *their* best, have always known better. They don't think in five-year plans but of eternity. They know that quality, the right way, the truth, will prove itself in the end, if, and it's a big if, enough people practise it always and without fail. They also know that they personally may not live to see the results. No matter.

Jesus knew this, even if some of His disciples didn't. Great scientists, great artists and great leaders know it; so do very ordinary people, like my father I think, unappreciated by me in his lifetime but, thinking about him now, he stood for quality and truth, and remains a greater influence on me now than when he lived.

Most of us are 'ordinary' – but 'quality', 'the truth', 'our best' are always possible. It's just difficult. Very difficult. Why bother? Faith, I suppose. Faith that that is actually our purpose in life. You could say, 'It's the will of God.' That's all. That's enough.

Fifty Thousand Hours

'A job is a job is a job,' said the trade unionist, 'and there aren't enough of them, that's all there is to it.'

Unfortunately it isn't. Jobs aren't actually getting fewer, any more, but they *are* getting smaller, and that's going to cause new dilemmas for business and especially for the good business which sees its workers as its continuing responsibility and not just as costs in the accounts.

Think of it this way. We used to sign on for 100,000 hours of work in our lifetime. That's 47 hours a week (including overtime) for 47 weeks a year for 47 years of life. Today more and more people are working 35 hours a week in offices for 45 weeks a year for what may only be 32 years of their life (from say twenty or twenty-two to their early fifties). Believe it or not that works out to be 50,000 hours. Without really noticing it we have cut the job in half, particularly for those young people starting work today.

50,000 hours instead of 100,000 hours. That makes you

wonder what we are going to be doing in the other 50,000 hours and what we are going to be living on. It means that firms have to start wondering whether they are morally obliged to keep people on until they are sixty-five even if they don't need them any more, or whether they ought to pay them the same pension if they leave at fifty-five instead of sixty-five, whether indeed any business can any longer afford to offer anyone a job and a full pension for life, if that life is going to last another twenty-five years beyond retirement.

Maybe it's more fundamental than that. Maybe we won't be 'retiring' at all, just working differently. I asked an old farmer near here what the difference was between farming at seventy and farming at fifty. 'No difference,' he said, 'just slower!' We will work because we have to, for the money, and we'll work because we want to, for the companionship, for the feeling that we are needed, for the sense of worth that only work can give. It's just that the work will be different, and slower. Much of it will be part-time, for two or three days a week, or at hours of our choosing. Much of it will be effectively self-employment, doing bits and pieces of work for different clients. Some of it will be for money, some for free, some for love and some because someone has to do it, like the housework or the caring.

Good news or bad? Good news if you enjoy the work, because in the end it is work of some sort that gives point to life. 'All play and no work,' to reverse the traditional saying, 'makes Jack an empty boy.' Eden wouldn't have been a paradise for long if Adam and Eve had had no gardening to do. But it's bad news if the work means more drudgery and more slavery, working only to eat.

The challenge of the 50,000 hours is to turn them into an opportunity for everyone to create a better balance of the different sorts of work and leisure in the last third of our lives, the Third Age. Do that and I'll be happy to cut the word 'retirement' out of my dictionary!

Go and He Goeth Not

The man in the Bible whom I have sometimes secretly envied is the young officer who told Jesus, 'I say unto a man go and he goeth and to another come and he cometh.' It has never seemed to work quite like that for me.

I suspect that the President of the USSR would also envy the simplicity of that officer's world as he struggles to hold his own world together. But the President and the rest of us are going to have to learn new ways because no free person should have to put up with being ordered around today, unless they agree with the order and with the person giving it.

It doesn't make life easy. Some years ago, in despair at our inability to run the Business School, where I worked, in a business-like way, we accepted an offer of help from a successful manager who wanted, he said, to leave his business and apply his managerial talents to something different. He was put in charge of the administration of the teaching programmes and was appalled by the

disarray he found. He called a meeting of the professors
– but no one came! 'Why not?' he asked me. 'They
probably had other things to do,' I said. 'It's like an
invitation to a party, they come if they don't have a better
invitation. You will have to negotiate a date.' He did and
they came. He told them his new rules. One of them said
to him gently, 'Richard, you can't *tell* us what to do, you
can only *ask* us and see if we agree.'

'Oh, I see, it's participative management time, is it?' he
said. 'Well then *you* tell me how we ought to arrange
things.' 'No, Richard,' they said, 'that's your job not
ours; *you've* got to come up with a better idea and win our
approval or persuade us that this scheme really is the
best. That way we own it and will deliver it.' He groaned,
but learned to do it their way. He was surprised to find
how well it worked, with less cost, less friction and less
need for checking.

What it all means is that if you are a leader or a
manager you will have to earn your authority from the
very people over whom you will exercise it. We govern
only with the consent of the governed and manage with
the consent of the managed. It is the difference between
being *in* authority as that officer in the Bible was and
speaking *with* authority as Jesus is described by those
who believed in Him. It sounds like a tiny change of
preposition but it means a huge change in behaviour.

We should resist therefore the temptation to assume
authority and the power that is needed to back it. That
way lies management by fear, or by the secret police.
Earn the authority instead. The founder of Christianity
was, in the old allegory, tempted by the Devil to take the
power to change the world, but chose instead to earn his

authority the hard way, because only in that way would it last. It is sadly ironical that some of the institutions that later bore his name did not resist the same temptation.

They had to rule by fear. They did not last. Dictators around the world today should take note. We in our own organizations and families should take note. Authority has to be earned. I'm pleased to say.

Group-Think

Last week I went to stay with my mother-in-law. Now mothers-in-law aren't for staying with in the myth, but actually I greatly enjoy my time there. Not only does she ply me with excellent food and drink but I get to read her newspapers! That provides me with a very different view of Britain from the one which I normally get over breakfast. How strange to find that not everyone is arguing rationally about the Anglo-Irish agreement, economic forecasts or the latest business merger. What odd interests other people have!

The truth is that it's very good for me to be bereft of my normal newspapers. I have to start to think for myself. No pre-packaged set of opinions on the issues of the day are there to confirm my prejudice and tell me what to say. My comfort-zone removed. We are all quite good, I guess, at creating these comfort-zones – not just newspapers, but friends who think like us. It's what makes life predictable.

In the jargon of my profession it is called group-think, a state of affairs in which all around are of a common mind so that no one notices that the emperor is actually naked, or at least would never presume to say so. I shall always remember the fascinating research studies of the groups where all but one of the members are briefed beforehand to say that what is clearly the shorter of two lines seems to them to be the longer one, with the result that the one unbriefed member begins to doubt the evidence of his own eyes and will, in fact, usually agree with the majority!

It sounds bizarre. But it happens. I can think of too many times when I've nodded my head for the sake of a quiet life, when I've let myself be argued into agreeing to something which I know is wrong. A decent humility, you might say, or a respect for others. Too often it's just cowardice, or laziness – the comfort of group-think. Organizations are rife with group-think. They not only read the same newspapers, they wear the same clothes, tell the same jokes. They even glory in it, calling it 'shared values'. Shared values are great, of course, if the values are great.

But those shared values can also lull you into a sort of moral anaesthesia, where you find yourself agreeing too readily that the obvious way to deal with the fall in profits is to amputate a bit of the organization, that it's OK to fantasize your expenses because it's 'the un-written law of the firm', that you must cut yourself in on the action because 'everyone expects it'. Cocooned by like-minds we can drift into a moral swamp like the man who was amazed to find himself jailed for being what he thought was just a clever businessman.

Truth actually is important, I reckon; being true to

oneself, that is. Living a lie does not feel good and organizations which lie to themselves come to a distressingly predictable end. Best to remember the psalmist who reckoned heaven was for him 'who doeth the thing which is right and speaketh the truth from his heart', or to go with George Orwell who said that even if you are in a minority of one you aren't necessarily mad.

'Know yourself,' said the Greeks. 'Be yourself,' I would add. It may not be comfortable. It has to be better.

Three-Faced Justice

'A fair day's pay for a fair day's work'. That seems a sensible enough philosophy for a business to adopt. A just pay policy, you might say.

Unfortunately it isn't quite as simple as that, for justice has always been one of those good words that mean different things to different people, and so it is with the word 'fair'. What seems fair to one can seem discrimination to another.

One view of justice, for instance, is that it means giving everyone what they need. That seems right and proper but so does the other definition: giving everyone what they deserve. Under the first definition those in need are the first priority, under the second those who work hardest and best come first. It's an issue which has split politicians between left and right down the ages. Give them what they need pulls to the left. Give them what they deserve pulls to the right. There's even a third definition of justice, that it means giving everyone the same *unless* it is clear that giving someone a bit more benefits everyone; that is, giving special attention to the handicapped helps them to contribute to society, and, perhaps, giving great leaders big inducements benefits the rest of us.

What then is fair pay? Can it be right that one person be paid ten times more than another? 'Yes,' say some, 'if he produces ten times as much.' 'No,' say others, 'because no one needs ten times as much as another.' 'Yes,' say others, 'if that's what other people like him or her are getting.' It's the old justice problem again.

I can see why it seems perfectly fair to some that the chairman of a company gets a £100,000 increase when the foreman gets £270. I can also see why it will seem grotesquely unfair to others. 'Fair's fair' seems to beg an awful lot of questions. Nor can we leave it to the market. The market will tell us the going rate, which one might think would be the measure of what is deserved, one of the definitions of justice, but all markets are temporary and all are quirky or imperfect. It might be worth my while to pay the only plumber not on holiday in August an outrageous rate to mend my burst pipe, but that would not mean he deserves it. Markets, as they say, will tell you the price of anything and the value of nothing. Don't count on them for justice, that's for sure.

Justice, I think, wears different clothes in different circumstances. Robin Hood understood this – so does my entrepreneur friend who guarantees his employees a decent wage and a small share of the profits but takes for himself no wage but a large bonus when the good times come, trading security for risk. When you get it right I think you know you've got it right. Only remember that there's always another definition, another side to the coin. Or, to put it more crisply, in the words of the prophet Micah, 'Do justly, love mercy and walk humbly with your God.'

The Greener Grass

There is one very puzzling parable in the Bible, at least to me. Actually, there is more than one which perplexes but then parables are meant to be full of meanings and I can't claim to catch them all.

Well, this is the one about the farmer who hired some people to work on his land early one morning. As the day went on he hired a few more, and some right in the last hours of the day. Then when he came to pay them, he gave each of them the same amount, no matter how many hours they had worked. When the early birds grumbled at this, the farmer replied that he had paid *them* exactly what had been agreed and that if he chose to pay the same to the others that was due to the kindness of his heart and was no cause for them to complain.

When I first heard this story I felt that Jesus was condoning injustice *and* arbitrary pay policies. Then I learnt that the parable was about the generosity of God's love. But parables at their best carry personal messages and the message for me in this story is about the destructiveness of envy.

Some hold that envy is the spur to economic growth, and I guess that much of advertising is based on this belief. Dissatisfied souls try harder. It doesn't work that way with me. I want to pull down the others rather than climb up to them, just like the complaining labourers in the story, and when I can't I growl and rumble about the unfairness of life until self-righteous misery envelops me.

I feel that way when I see the tables which come out every year in the Sunday papers comparing typical British earnings. If you saw one recently, it would have had Britain's best-paid businessmen at the top with well over one million pounds a year, while professors and their ilk, like me, came a good two-thirds of the way down the list. Naturally I didn't linger long on those below me on the list; I looked spitefully and enviously at all those above me. Quite ruined that sunny Sunday afternoon.

Actually we don't even need the lists. Research shows that if organizations conceal their salary lists to stop people getting jealous then everybody makes their own guesses anyway about their colleagues and they always guess that the others are getting more than they really are. It's a sort of envious masochism in us and the result I have to say, is seldom new endeavours, seldom an end to any unfairness, just more unhappy people, just like the labourers in the parable.

So I have now resolved some things. I will try not to begrudge others their good luck in life but will wish them well with it. I will stop wondering about what might have been if I too had got in on those shares, if I had not sold the house five years ago, or left that job. I will not yearn for the grass on the other side of the fence which might be greener but seldom is, for I know, in my heart, that it is easier to walk down life's path if you look straight ahead and not over your shoulder at other people. It is certainly less depressing.

Organizations for Masochists

Thinking about it the other day, I realized that some of my unhappiest moments have been in organizations. Somehow it seems to be quite respectable to do things in organizations which you would never do in private life. I have had people insult me to my face in front of my colleagues. I have had my feelings rammed down my throat on the pretext that it would do me good, and have been required to do things which I didn't agree with because the organization wished it.

And then there are all those games which organizations play, the political battles over what we can spend, who works for whom, or who sits where, or is paid what. If, like me, you're not very good at fighting your own corner you can end up sitting in the little room at the end of the corridor, wondering what they're talking about in those meetings you weren't invited to, simmering with resentment and hurt.

In my worst moments I have thought that organizations were places designed to be run by sadists and staffed by masochists – and I'm not just talking about business, some of these things happened in the holiest of places with the nicest of people. Why is it, I wonder, that ninety per cent of us choose to work in these odd communities, if we have the choice? Why does it sometimes have to be so awful?

Well, it doesn't have to be like that. The best organizations to be in, it seems, are the busiest ones as long as they are being busy for someone else. The worst are those that are obsessed with their own innards.

You know how it is when you say 'How do you do?' to someone and they insist on telling you, in gruesome medical detail, how they *do* do, or rather, how parts of them do not do, and you realize that this is someone obsessed with themselves, neurotic, boring and probably useless to anyone else. The interesting people are often the healthy ones, those who are so absorbed in other things and other people that they haven't time to worry about themselves.

Well, it seems to be the same with organizations. The healthiest are those which exist for others, not for themselves. Show me a business, or a school, or a church that is preoccupied with its customers or clients, determined to do its best for them, and not just to survive for the sake of surviving, and I'll bet you that they don't have time for too many committees, for forms, for politicking or for nit picking about mistakes. Those are the organizations which are fun to be in, which give you room to be yourself, to express yourself, to grow.

We all, it seems, need a *purpose beyond ourselves* to make the best of ourselves. Lose sight of that purpose and we get obsessed with our navels, turned in on ourselves. St

Augustine said it was the most destructive of sins, but it's one that's easy to slip into, to be fascinated by our bodies and forget why they are there. The Minister was being shown around the new hospital and said to the administrator how impressed he was. 'Ah,' the administrator said, 'but you should have seen it before the patients arrived, it was fantastic then.' They told it on the comedy show *Yes, Minister* but it has the feel of truth.

It may sound odd for a Professor of Business to say this but I reckon that our organizations could do with a deal more loving, a bit more forgiveness and a lot more faith in other people. Such things, however, in organizations as in life, are only possible if we feel we are in the grip of something bigger than ourselves and so can lose ourselves in others.

'Where there is no vision the people perish,' said the psalmist. Quite so. And organizations too.

Sign It!

I was pleased to see an advert for a smart Swiss watch the other day, not because I need a smart Swiss watch (the cheaper the smarter these days, isn't it, in watches?) but because the advert said that the watch would come with a signature on it, the signature not of the customer but of the man or woman who made it.

That's nice, I thought – the worker has a name at last, because I remembered that when *I* started work my office door had the name of the department in metal screwed into the wood, but just below it was a slot with a plastic slip which you could slide in and out. My name was on the plastic slip. It was quite obvious, even to me, that it wouldn't make much difference to the door, the office or to anyone if someone else's name on another slip of plastic was slipped into that slot. I was discovering the real meaning of the sociological term 'a role occupant'. I was the human being who for the time being was filling that role. I wasn't really or fully *me*, I was the inheritor of a job description.

Now I know well enough that you can't run an organization without defining the jobs that need to be done, setting out areas of responsibility and patterns of accountability. Those are all essential. But it's wrong, morally wrong, I believe, to treat people as if they were interchangeable human parts. They aren't completely interchangeable. It does make a difference which name goes into that slot in the office door. We know it does. We shouldn't pretend it doesn't.

It's pervasive, this role-occupant stuff – that's what worries me. 'What do you do?' we ask people at a party, but we don't really want to hear everything they do, we want to hear the name of their role, their job title, their organization – then we've got a box to put them in and the exchange of pleasantries can continue without anyone really getting to know anyone. Roles, job titles, organizational boxes can in fact be devices to stop people knowing each other, sorts of shields which we carry round in front of us.

It used not to be like that. The worker was a craftsman or artisan, there was a signature of a kind to everything, whether it was made by the carpenter, shaped by the blacksmith or tended by the gardener. Maybe, helped by the new technology the tradition is creeping back as with my watchmaker, or with the credit lists on the TV programmes which list all the names of the people involved. It does make a difference, having a name. One of the nicest things about writing books, I find, is having your name on the front.

It means that I have signed my work, and what I sign for I'm responsible for, and accountable for. Signed work tends therefore to be better work. It's more important than that. Putting names before job titles means that we expect the name to make a difference to the job, and that's what we were all born for, to make a difference to this world of ours, we hope for the better.

There ought to be a law, forcing each of us to sign our work. On second thoughts, why do we need a law when it's so obviously both sensible and right?

Subsidiarity

Are you like me – do you apologize to strangers for other people's problems – the traffic, the weather, the state of English cricket? More seriously, do you yearn to take over your children's problems and solve them for them? I do. I've also tried to run an organization single-handed to save other people their worries – and perhaps because, more honestly, I thought I would do it better. And I'm not the only one. I know people who attract other people's problems like a magnet; I know managers who see it as their duty to solve all their subordinates' problems for them and I know very caring people who want to save their ageing parents from any decision at all.

It's well-meant, I'm sure, most of the time, but I've come to see that it won't do, most of the time. Stealing people's problems means stealing their choices and, unless they are totally incapable, that's denying them some of the responsibility that is their due. The Catholic Church, I find, has a word for it – Subsidiarity – try saying that late at night! A papal encyclical explained what it meant. 'It is an injustice, a grave evil and a disturbance of right order for a larger and higher organization to arrogate to itself functions which can be performed efficiently by smaller and lower bodies.' If you didn't realize before that delegation was a moral duty you do now!

Actually, that's not quite right. Delegation suggests that you are taking part of your responsibility and giving it to someone else. Subsidiarity says that the responsibility is theirs in the first place and shouldn't be delegated upwards unless they are incapable. It seems that giving away your problems and your choices is just as bad as shouldering ones that aren't properly yours.

Strangely, perhaps, it's often tempting to give away your choices. When I was in a multinational company I was quite happy for them to tell me which country to go to and which job to do – that left me free to complain if I didn't like it. Indeed, I know organizations where problems fly upwards like sparks from a fire, each layer passing the decision to the one above lest they get it wrong. And isn't it lovely, sometimes, to be given a problem, to be the expert, the responsible one, carrying the burdens of the world, or at least of the family or the firm? And isn't it hard to say 'no', to say that he or she must decide, it's their responsibility, when you know that you could do it better?

I confess that I never find it easy to refuse a problem but I've come to learn that it's often kinder to hand it back, because it's only by managing their own choices that people learn to grow and be free.

The religious equivalent of delegating upwards is, I

suspect, 'leave it to the Holy Spirit'. Well, I don't know about you, but I believe that God also believes in subsidiarity and that while He is always there to support and inspire He wouldn't dream of taking from us our right to choose. Choices, in fact, are our privilege, although they come disguised as problems, and stealing people's choices is wrong.

Picture-Framing

I once started a senior management course by asking the assembled managers what lay at the heart of their job. 'Taking decisions,' they said. 'Right,' I replied. 'Why don't you each come back here on Monday with your biggest decision of the week and we'll discuss it.' Next Monday the first manager said, rather shamefacedly, 'Last week was rather odd, I didn't actually take anything that could be called a big decision.' Neither it appeared had any of the others. 'An odd week, then?' I asked. No, in fact a very normal week. The truth is that leaders don't only, or even mostly, take decisions in well-run systems.

What do they do then? Well they spend a lot of time picking the people who pick the people who do make the decisions. I asked a Head once how he got the school to be the way he wanted it. 'I pick the Heads of Departments and the Heads of Houses,' he said, 'and then I wait five years.' But sometimes you don't have five years, and sometimes you find that your Heads have already been picked for you, or that you don't have an awful lot of choice. So what else do leaders do? What should the Chairman, the President, or the Prime Minister be worrying about? Reframing, I would suggest; not paintings but pictures in the mind. Good leaders are adept at reframing problems, at putting old facts into new bottles, at reconceptualizing the familiar so that new solutions leap up. Here's one example. A friend recently criticized an acquaintance of ours for bringing, as she put it, another bastard into the world. The word startled me. I hadn't heard it in its literal sense for ten years. Whoever coined the phrase 'single-parent family' had reframed the whole situation so that new behaviours, new attitudes and new laws became not only possible but obvious. There's an unsung leader there, somewhere. Do that for a whole nation or an organization and you set a sort of chemical reaction underway.

Mahatma Gandhi, to go to the other extreme, was a great reframer, turning a resistance movement from active to passive and so making it ultimately invincible. John Kennedy likewise – no great decision-maker he, but his reframing energized a nation and part of the world. I wish we could train more people to be great reframers but I fear that, even in the best of our business schools, we can only develop it a little if it's actually there. Those who have it are blessed indeed, and greatly needed.

This is the real challenge to any President, of a country or a business, to do more creative reframing for their world, to create a picture of the task which gives meaning to existence and endeavour. But it is also a challenge for all those, in politics or management, in education or in the media, who aspire to lead others, for management is just a tug-of-war when the picture has no frame, and politics a petty squabble. I sometimes think that we forget that Jesus Himself took few decisions, gave few commands, did very little. If you wrote out His CV it would read like a failure. We know now, of course, that He was reframing the picture – and changing the world. There's hope there for the rest of us; it is not our own dull CV that will be remembered but the pictures we reframed for others.

Chinese Contracts

Last week we sold our fridge. I thought the chap seemed very happy when he signed the cheque. In fact, come to think of it, he didn't even try to bargain. Oh dear, I thought, I've priced it too low. I've failed again. Or had I?

I remembered then my days long ago in Singapore when I was selling lubricating oils to the Chinese. We used to celebrate each deal with a twelve course meal – delicious. But it was when I brought out the formal company contracts for them to sign that they started to laugh out loud.

'Now why do you want those bits of paper?' they would say. 'What kind of contract is it if you need a judge and law courts to make it stick?!' To the Chinese businessman, you see, a good deal was one which was *bound* to be self-enforcing, because both parties gained from it equally, and both parties lost if it went wrong. Formal contracts were superfluous, even a bit suspicious.

'Oh,' I used to say, 'it's just an old English ritual which

my bosses insist on.' But it wasn't just an old English ritual; it was an entirely different way of looking at the world. I was brought up in that different way, believing that a 'good deal' was a deal which I won, where I came away with more than the other chap and where, if need be, I kept him to his bargain by the threat of the law. The Chinese way, of a good deal being one where both sides win, was a very strange idea – but it worked!

I can't help thinking about all this whenever the Americans start talking to the Russians again, or when managements sit down with their unions, or when my sadly divorcing friends go to talk to their respective lawyers. Which philosophy of a 'good deal' will prevail, I always wonder. But I also come up against it myself every day, and not just when I'm selling fridges. Only last week I was also arguing with some publishers over a contract, I was negotiating with my daughter over the use of the car, and I wanted the neighbour to repair the fence – all 'deals' to be arranged. Which philosophy should I work to? Would I boast about the way I had got it all my way, or would I be pleased that we were both pleased?

If you think about it – it's pretty fundamental stuff. After all, if a good deal means a deal in which both parties win then 'compromise' isn't something to be ashamed of, it's right and proper. It means being serious about the other person's needs and wishes, it means seeing things from the other side of the fence and sympathizing with their view; and you can't do that, I find, unless you like them, or try to.

'Love your enemies,' I was told when I was young. It seemed daft, then, and not the way to go about winning.

Now – grown up at last – I'm not so sure. If good deals, deals that work and stick, mean deals where both sides win then you have to start by genuinely wanting him or her, or them, to win as well as you; and that's not a bad start to loving. What kind of world would it be, I wonder, if we all genuinely wanted our opposites to do as well as we did in every situation? Naïve? Perhaps, because mankind is fallible, but it's an interesting idea, it's been around now for two thousand years and to the Chinese it's also good business; but it has to be bad news for lawyers!

Entrepreneurs All

I revel in my Irish ancestry and take every opportunity to go to that lovely country. Last year my wife and I found ourselves in the Irish Midlands, in the bog country. We stayed Sunday night in one of those lovely dilapidated Georgian houses in the middle of the fields which had been turned into a guest house by an enterprising young couple. But when we came down the next morning to the promised Irish breakfast there was no one there. The shutters were drawn, the rooms all dark and empty. Our innkeepers had overslept! Undismayed, we raided their fridge, made some tea and had our breakfast, the lady of the house appearing just as we were leaving, billowing with apologies. 'We had a lovely night and we over-slept,' she said and, of course, we forgave her.

It was all pleasingly Irish and rather appropriate because we were going to a conference on do-it-yourself business, or entrepreneuring. One of Ireland's largest employers was planning to turn most of its workers into independent businessmen, selling their product back to the firm but as entrepreneurs, not employees, responsible now for their own destinies. It is happening all over.

'Great,' said some, rubbing their hands at the prospect, but others looked glum. Freedom and responsibility, even for oneself, can be frightening. I know how they felt, those glum ones. I used to be an in-tray person myself once, a cog in someone else's machine, useful I hope, but passive, not fully alive and certainly not in control of my destiny. But that was how things were meant to be, I felt, and I was not one for rocking the boat, not in those days anyway.

Then one day I read the first chapter of Paul's letter to the Galatians. In it Paul tells the Galatians that when he had his blinding vision on the road to Damascus he went straight off to Arabia to preach to the gentiles, without speaking to any human being and did not check in to Head Office in Jerusalem for fourteen years, apart from a brief private chat with Cephas after three. 'What I write is plain truth,' he says, as if they wouldn't credit it. 'Before God I am not lying.'

They would not have put up with him in my company, I thought. And then I reflected, if Paul, why not me? But then I would have checked in to Jerusalem and been given an in-tray to deal with, or, on Paul's previous record, probably been shown the door. Paul just got on and did it because he felt he had to.

In that sense Paul was, I think, the true entrepreneur, for entrepreneurs don't just belong in business. They are all the people who make things happen and don't just wait for them to happen, in *all* parts of life. People like us, potentially. God may not speak to us as vividly as He did to Paul but I believe that each one of us has something that we are meant to do, some difference that we are meant to make, somewhere. When we know what it is, we cannot wait around for things to happen; we should *make* them happen. Like Paul did. Like entrepreneurs do.

Gyroscopes for Morals

Have you heard of the latest best-selling business book from America? It's called *The Ethics of Wall Street* and it consists of 168 blank pages!

It is a sick joke. But it reminds me that the moral dilemmas of the financial world may be some sort of parable for the rest of us, and indeed that part of our censorious attitude is fuelled by the thought that 'there but for the grace of God go I,' or, to be rather more blunt that 'I wouldn't mind having a few of their dilemmas myself!!'

Let's face it, it's a different world up there in the City or in Wall Street. One has to remember, for instance, that the international money deals which the City makes add up, in the course of a year, to more than all the physical goods and services traded by this country. More than, did I say? Much more than. In fact, I'm told, thirty times more than.

But then money is used in two ways in that world. Some of it is ordinary money of the sort we all use to pay the wages and buy the groceries, but most of it is money as a commodity, money which people buy and sell, money money you might say. It must sometimes be very confusing to move from talking money money to ordinary money in the middle of a hectic day and it's easy to understand how one might calculate a percentage in money money terms instead of in ordinary money. Nor would that matter too much if that money money didn't just occasionally end up as *real* money in a bank account or as a turbo-charged Porsche in the garage.

That's the problem, I think. One loses touch with what's real. It's like flying a plane in fog. You don't know whether you're upright or not unless there's a gyroscope in the cabin. Lose touch with reality and you lose your moral gyroscope and do things which in the cold light of day would *amaze* you. It happens in war, of course, but more ordinarily it can happen in any intense working atmosphere, in a hothouse advertising agency and in many a sales office. Shut out reality and you can lose your moral balance – do *anything* to get that sale.

Where do you look for the gyroscope then? Not to the people around you, because they're in the same hot-house, like the eminent banker who, at the height of the City scandals, declared that insider dealing was a victimless crime. Not to Laws, I feel, which deal only with extreme situations and usually after they have happened.

No, there *is* no gyroscope out there. We each have to look for it inside ourselves – and it's always there. I believe *that* because I believe that the spirit or essence of God is in each and every one of us whether we formally acknowledge it or not. Get in touch with that spirit and you are in touch with truth. As a city banker said to a bishop the other day: 'Don't preach at us, help us to find spirituality' – and it might be worth a Porsche to him to find his soul again.

The 'They' Syndrome

'They really ought to do something about it,' said the taxi driver the other night, pointing at the traffic jammed up ahead of us. Who 'they' were or what they should do was, naturally, not specified. It was just another example of what I have come to call the 'they' syndrome – after the woman who told me that she was having to move out of her married quarters with her child because she was separating from her army husband. 'Where are you going to live then?' I asked. 'They haven't told me,' she said. 'Who are they?' I said, curious. She looked at me as if I was peculiarly stupid. 'They haven't told me who they are, have they?' she said witheringly.

I shouldn't be so scathing. I spent ten years in a big company waiting patiently for them to shape my life while *they* deplored my lack of gumption in taking no initiatives. And I'm often wondrously tolerant of expert authority. When the doctor told me that they knew nothing about the cause of my virus and could not cure it, I murmured 'thank you', hugged my pain to myself and went away strangely reassured that 'they' were no wiser than me!

A proper deference, you might say. Sheer escapism is more often the truth – and it's very pervasive. Any organization will have its 'theys' who, everyone hopes, are taking care of the future, although, when pressed, no one is quite sure who 'they' are. It does let the rest of us nicely off the hook; lazily, passively we wait, for someone else.

I think that a lot of it is all to do with religion, but religion tragically misunderstood. 'Almighty God,' we pray, and Almighty He is, but that doesn't mean that He's our general factotum, sorting everything out for us. No, the excitement of Christianity for me is its insistence that God became Man, that God works through us, that I can't leave it to Him, that He is in fact in me. Frightening when you think about it but, actually, it's what gives life its meaning and its purpose. I would never want to think of myself as a predetermined doll, going through the motions in the hope of Nirvana at the end.

I suppose I take what's called a high view of Man, of mankind, that is. I go along with St John who said that the divine seed dwells in us, and also with Athanasius (he of the creed) who said, 'He was humanized that we might be deified.' I refuse to be what C. S. Lewis said I should be – a small dirty object in the presence of God – that's where the 'they' syndrome starts.

Take the high view and you give power to yourself, more things become possible, I find, problems turn out to conceal opportunities, blocks turn into stepping-stones – well, most of the time. It's worth a go anyway, so why not believe in yourself for a change, and stop delegating upwards. He doesn't like it, nor should 'they'!

Jesus was Lame

April is the time for daffodils and for grass which grows too quickly. It is also, for some of us, the month for conferences.

Oh those conferences! Shut up in an hotel with a gaggle of people, most of them strangers, stooping to peer at each other's chests as we try to read our labels. And at every conference I seem to go through the same cycle. As soon as I arrive depression deepens. Who are all those people? So imposing, so in command, intimidating almost. So glamorous, stars in their firmament. How can I compete? Yet most of them look depressingly boring, ugly even, at first sight. No way do I want to be marooned with these people.

Coward as I am, however, I don't escape. And always by the end the miracle has started to happen. The people now look different. That one who looked so imposing was after all just a shy soul hiding behind grim lips. The dumpy one in the ill-fitting suit was a bit of a genius with a lovely twist of humour. There are no ugly people now.

Just individuals with different faces. Appearances are deceptive. Of course. But I think that there is more to it than that.

One of the nicest stories I've heard from the early Christian tradition has it that Jesus was lame. True or not I want to believe it. I would like to believe too that if He had lived a little bit longer He might also have been bald, like me. If Jesus was lame and maybe going bald, then no one mentioned it because no one noticed. Just imagine; those gospel writers, writing about the most important man who ever lived and not one of them tells us what He looked like. So if Jesus was lame and no one noticed it, why? Because of what I believe Keats meant when he wrote: 'Beauty is truth, truth beauty.' Just that. Truth is beauty, beauty truth. The truth of who you are will always shine more strongly than what you look like.

Jesus was lame and no one noticed. I find the idea very comforting as I stand in the bathroom in the morning, peering yet again at that drearily familiar face. Only be *true* and no one will notice the body I inhabit.

Only be true – true to the best in oneself, true to one's beliefs, I suppose, true to what the Roman poet Lucretius called the essence of things. It's the secret of the meaning of life, I think, this truth – and of death come to that, when real truth comes to some for the first time. Only be true. But oh, how difficult it is – even in a conference with a label on my chest telling me who I am supposed to be.

Horizontal Fast-Tracks

Each year the BBC runs a competition in which listeners are asked to nominate and vote for the title 'Best of British Youth'. There is always a short-list of heroines and heroes who have defied life's odds to do good and notable deeds in their communities, often after failing their formal studies.

It all goes to strengthen my conviction that we are crazy to try to categorize people too soon, to fit them into predetermined slots. Character, happily, will keep breaking out.

The youngsters on the BBC list have, by their determination, found a niche where they can shine and can contribute. Even if *this* niche doesn't last forever they will know *forever* that life has meaning. Too many of their generation must doubt that. Too many must see little point in life and no niches anywhere.

It was when I was in Japan to find out how they developed their young managers that they told me about their horizontal fast-tracks. When the new recruits join the organization they switch them from job to job in their first five years – the better they learn the faster they move – but horizontally, not upwards, like we do. 'Why do you do this?' I asked. 'It's obvious,' they replied, which clearly it wasn't! It is not decreed that we should know our destiny or our talents at sixteen or even eighteen. All people should have different roles, in different places with different people to find out what their special contribution can be, to make their first mistakes in safety and to learn a nice variety of skills. 'Is it not like that with you?' they said.

No. But it's a neat idea and not just for managers. Would it not be a better world if we could guarantee to *all* young people a protected horizontal track for three years or so after school or college, a time to find a slot that suited and a skill that pleased? They would need the proper training, of course, to fill each slot and help to find the confidence to move along the track. But we could do that, are already doing it in places.

It would be great for the economy, I bet, for we would once again have a workforce equal to the best, but it is not these utilitarian things that concern me most this morning. I see it as a moral duty, a charge upon us, their elders, to give to everyone the chance to find their niche in life and their talents as early as may be. It has to be a moral duty if you believe with me that there is for each one of us a God-given purpose in this world; for *each* of us, uniquely, and not just for the favoured few.

Find that purpose and that special niche is another matter. Few are granted the shaft of light that struck Paul on the Damascus road, and even he was well into his first career. God's purposes need human hands to take effect.

Let me put it this way – stealing people's futures is wrong, even if we do it by neglect.

SOCIETY

On Planting a Walnut Tree

Earlier this year I planted a walnut tree. It's a strange feeling, planting walnut trees. You know that you are never going to see that tree looking as a walnut tree should, old and gnarled and venerable and full of nuts. Some day, perhaps, your grandchildren, or more likely some stranger's grandchildren, will look up and say, 'Doesn't that walnut look great,' or will curse it when the nuts get in the way of the lawnmower. They won't thank you or curse you – they won't even think of there being a you, someone who once consciously decided to plant that tree in that place. So why was I doing it? I won't see it grown up; no one will thank me for it or remember me for it. I guess I planted it because it just seemed right and would seem right in the days after I was gone. It was, I must admit, a good feeling. I wondered why such an irrational act felt so good. It set me thinking.

I wondered first why so little of the rest of my life had this kind of perspective. I was, most of the time, more like a sower of annual flowers, looking for results this summer, or at best a planter of shrubs which have a three-year pay-off. Yet I remembered the head of a family business telling me that the great family businesses were great partly because they found it natural to 'think beyond the grave'. Their successors would be their children and their children's children. It was easier therefore to take decisions which would not pay off in their time but only in the next generation. This gave them, he said, the sense of perspective, and of long-term strategy, which so many businesses find it so hard to cultivate.

I remembered, too, a discussion about the dilemmas of modern politicians who live with the constant need to win the next election which is on average only two-and-a-bit years away, yet have, on taking office, to decide on policies which may not produce results for ten years or more. 'Who,' asked someone, 'is looking after our grandchildren when those who govern us are looking after the next election? Is it right, for instance, to build up a huge financial deficit today in order to create more jobs, which is effectively borrowing from the grandchildren to keep the grandparents comfortable?'

'Thinking beyond the grave'. It's a nice phrase. Living now so that others later can live more abundantly. Life after death, but *others'* lives after *your* death. Perhaps that is part of what Christianity is really all about.

Blame it on the Greeks

'I can't stand those dark December mornings,' I said to someone yesterday. 'But just think,' she replied, 'how many sunrises you get to see.'

'Oh, don't be so twee,' was my gut reaction, although I was naturally too polite, or perhaps too timorous, to say so.

She was right for all that, but very un-British. It really isn't done to look on the bright side. Britain is the only country I know where a constant improvement in our standard of living is always referred to as a relative decline. Only in Britain is second-best an insult not a compliment. Only here is the golden age somewhere in the past. Only in Britain is it more seemly to celebrate a close defeat than a victory. They had a great party on the British yacht *White Crusader*, I heard, after she was knocked out of the America's Cup, but we almost apologize when we occasionally win a Test Match.

Come to think of it, success is almost a dirty word in this culture while even achievement sounds a bit pompous. I remember once in my youth, when I won a scholarship, I locked myself in the school lavatory for three hours for fear of the teasing I would get! On a more elevated plane, companies in America *boast* of how much of their success they pass on to the community or to charity whilst we feel that such things are best done, well, quietly, or by individuals. Too much bounty is too much boasting.

I put it all down to the Ancient Greeks, who have been infecting our educational system for centuries. Don't get too bumptious, said the Greeks, lest you make the gods jealous and they strike you down. Hubris, they called it, or the pride that comes before a fall. Best be humble, or pretend to be, and keep others humble too. If your subordinate, or your daughter, does well just make it clear that she could have done better. Develop a league table mentality so that only one lot ever wins and most feel more like losers, that way the gods won't be jealous. Oh, and remember, praise corrupts, so ration it. It's all very decent but very depressing.

I'd like to see us shuck off those Ancient Greeks and try another god. One who is never jealous, who wants a world where everyone can win, at something, who sets high standards but forgives mistakes; a culture where celebration is OK, where joy is part of life and heaven still ahead. It would be a quiet revolution of course, but isn't that what life ought to be all about?

A Work Mixer Please!

'It is simple idolatry,' said the man at the bar, 'that's all it is.' Actually, I think he meant *idleness* because he was banging on about the iniquity of the great Christmas/New Year shutdown which grips the British nation once a year; although of course he *may* have been making a rather subtle theological point about pagan festivals, graven images and so forth. Whatever he meant it set me thinking.

Is it idleness, this long holiday, I wondered, and is it all decadent – the sign of a nation in the last stages of decline, the final collapse of the work ethic?

I'm not so sure. I don't believe that we are now so much less virtuous because we no longer work eighty-hour weeks in miserable fields and factories, no longer take just one day off for holy days and none for holidays, or drop dead where we work instead of retiring. It is not *long* work that God and Calvin wanted but *effective* work.

Indeed it is my dream that one day in this land of ours we could have more because we produced more. It wouldn't require an economic miracle, just a lot of efficiency. If that were to happen then the Christmas break would be a sign not of decadence but of civilization, a reminder that life was never intended to be all work and certainly not all paid work.

Recreation, better pronounced re-creation, has to be part of that fuller life. Even God rested. But we also need the other sort of work, the work we do for free and I hope with love, tending children, minding houses, caring for neighbours. Gift work is the pleasing term they use. To Thomas Aquinas, it is the best work.

Sadly, right now, the parts have separated out. Some there are who have too much time for recreation so that it is anything but re-creation. We call them unemployed. Another lot gets all the gift work – UDWs they're called; yes UDWs – Unpaid Domestic Workers, an accurate title you might agree, all those of working age who choose not to seek for paid work. Honoured of God they may be but they go unrecognized by society although there are over five million such in Britain today. *They* might well say that gift work carried to extremes is no gift any longer but a chore.

And then there's all the paid work, with ever fewer people working ever longer hours instead of the other way round. It was Mark Twain who once said, ironically, that if work was such hot stuff the rich would have hogged it long ago. They have, Mr Twain, they have.

Pray God, I say, for a blending machine. A separated society will soon go sour. Man that is made in God's image needs a taste of each of those three parts. When that has happened, for each and *all* of us, then, and only then, can we truly say that our Christmas break is a *just* reward for a just society.

The Antigone Principle

I still remember the astonished looks on the faces of one lot of managers when they went into the classroom for the first session of their course. On each desk was a nice fat volume called *Understanding Company Accounts*. That was all right. They expected that. But on top of it was a much slimmer book – *Antigone* by Sophocles. 'It's OK,' I said. 'It may be a Greek play but it's in translation and it's your homework for tonight.'

They wondered what kind of liberal arts course they had wandered into but later that night they began to understand. Sophocles' play is about the dilemma of Antigone whose brother has been killed by her uncle Creon in a battle for the control of Thebes. Creon had won and had issued an edict that her brother's body was not to be buried but was to lie outside the walls to be picked at by crows and vultures. Anyone who attempted to give him the rites of burial would die. Everything in Antigone screamed out that she must give the last rites to her brother. It was her overwhelming religious duty.

Creon said, in his avuncular way, don't be silly, your first duty is to obey the law. Was it? Or was her first duty to do what was right even if it meant death? There was no comfortable answer – this was a Greek tragedy after all.

I did not need to remind those managers the next day that company accounts were not the most difficult problem they would face at work. More difficult at times is knowing when you should do far more than the company lays down, when you should overturn a rule or, in effect, break a bad law, the times in other words when principles and standards become more important than a quiet life.

Some people use Antigone's argument to justify disregarding laws or taxes which they feel unfair. Customs duties are fair game, it seems, and so was the poll tax when it was first introduced in Britain, but that is to belittle Antigone's dilemma. Don't make a moral principle out of an administrative duty, Jesus said once long ago, or, more grandiloquently, 'Render unto Caesar the things that are Caesar's and to God the things that are God's.' He had a point, I think.

Customs duties and poll taxes, however, are easy dilemmas, and so, in a way, was Antigone's life or death decision. It's the smaller humdrum things that provide a bigger test. Should we at work, for instance, tolerate dirty, unhealthy even dangerous conditions when we know that if we complain we'll be told to lump it or leave? Should we just stand by and let a colleague suffer the persistent nudge-nudge of sexual harassment, or should we make a stand?

Antigone knew that life would not be worth living if she was not true to her beliefs and her standards. My worry is that too often I, and I suspect a few others, are only too ready to settle for that life not worth living. Whenever I do, I know that I have diminished myself and, in a sense, denied my God.

The Point of Principle

Not long ago I was sent another of those so-called personalized letters offering me the choice of a video-recorder, I think it was, cash or a holiday for two if I went along to a sales pitch for a holiday time-sharing scheme. You've probably had one too – I think their mailing lists must be based on the telephone directory – and you probably threw it away. I'm afraid I'm a sucker and on an earlier occasion I went along and was subjected to their high-pressure sales pitch. I managed to escape, I'm relieved to say, with my cheque-book untouched *and* with my bribe – that time it was a miniature carriage clock.

Yes bribe – for that was what it was, and I had succumbed. The world seems increasingly full of bribes these days, quiz games on telly, coupons on packets, golden hellos in the City. Even the company takeover game has turned into a bribery competition for share-holders, with not much obvious thought or attention paid to the people who work in them or to the products they make. In effect every company in Britain and America is now potentially for sale, to someone, if the bribe is big enough and the bankers brave enough. You might even argue that the big share-issues that went with the privatization of state industries in Britain were intended to bribe us all into the stock market, for good or ill.

It has to be distorting. Company boards now have to spend more time protecting their shares than managing their business, shareholders become traders not owners, we as individuals find ourselves pulled this way and that by enterprising seducers until we don't know which way is what. The world, for some people, seems overfull of choices.

I wouldn't want to do away with the choices. I feel far sorrier for the people with no choices at all than for those bewildered by them. So it is ultimately up to us.

'Choices are easier if you have principles,' I found myself saying rather pompously to my son the other day. 'What principles?' he said. 'Yours?' 'No,' I said, ignoring the implied question, '*yours*, the only ones which actually stick are the ones you work out for yourself.'

My son's dilemma was whether he should go on welfare, take the dole, while he was working full-time, but for no money, trying to build up his dance band and therefore not actually free for other work. 'It's what everyone does,' he said. 'It's accepted practice. Having principles does not make the choice any easier.'

Yes it does, but first you have to decide whether to follow your principles or 'accepted practice'. Why lose out, one feels, when everyone else is eating cake? That's the tough decision – principles or accepted practice? After that it's easy.

It would be nice, I think, if it once again became a compliment to say that someone was a man or woman of principle. It would stop us being slaves to accepted practice, make many of our choices much easier and would have saved me two hours of bombast and a miniature carriage clock.

The Lure of the Noughts

One week a property developer walked into a friend of mine's house and offered him ten times what he had paid for it eight years before – more than he had earned in his whole life so far and just for sitting there!

Yes, this was London and at a time when thousands in the Midlands and the North could not get *any* offer at all for their houses.

Then I heard of a young man being offered a six figure 'golden hello' just to make a job offer in a bank rather more tempting, on top of a starting salary of £60,000. Could he really be *that* good? – when millions, as we know, couldn't get a job at all. Those were the days!

And at that time, too, there was my young godchild, just qualified with a good degree in engineering from a top university; she rang me to tell me of her first job – with a prestigious firm of stockbrokers. 'But what about the engineering?' I asked, when I had congratulated her. 'Oh, no one can afford to be an engineer these days,' she said. 'I'm getting twice the money plus bonuses.'

Temporary imperfections in the free market – that's what they said they were, and they will correct themselves in time. Well, maybe, but it takes a long time and in the meantime can such huge imperfections be right?

It's my friends that I worry about. You can't blame them or people like them, for taking advantage of their luck. Money is *not* the root of all evil – St Paul was careful to say that it was the *love* of money which was the problem. But I wonder if you really can see straight with all those noughts in front of you, still disentangle right from wrong, above all still be *true to yourself* in spite of the numbers. My house-owning friend is thinking of moving to a house which is quite out of character in a world where he won't fit. The banker may find himself locked into a ghetto, a slave to his job and a bore to his friends, burnt out at forty. My godchild, engineer that she is, may hate the wheeler-dealing City but be too rich to leave. I hope none of this happens of course, but I've seen too many people trapped this way into living a lie – the worst of sins St Augustine said.

We can't abolish money, and I wouldn't want to. Indeed we need lots more of it. It is the fuel of civilization. The trouble is that when the fuel goes where it isn't meant to, it can get messy and dangerous. I just hope and pray that those who have the money can set light to it personally, and that they won't lose their souls for the name of the game. It was this I believe that St Matthew had in mind when he recorded Jesus as saying: 'Blessed are the poor in *spirit* for they shall see heaven.' Is there time enough, I wonder, in this busy money-world for the things of the spirit? If not, then we should make time if we want to stay true to ourselves in the midst of the numbers.

The Missing Words

Education in Britain in the end was something too important to be left to teachers. There is now a national curriculum enshrined in an Educational Reform Act (the new ERA they joke). Parliament has decided what our children should be taught.

It would no doubt disturb the splendid legal phraseology but I would like to suggest that they insert somewhere in that Act three old-fashioned words – curiosity, forgiveness and love – words which, to my mind, still lie at the heart of all learning.

I can tell you that they weren't much in evidence in my school, years ago. Curiosity there was called impertinence. If I learnt one lesson it was that all problems had already been defined and solved. The teacher knew the answer, so don't ask, memorize. Forgiveness? Why, to forgive was soft. So, if you erred, don't get caught. If you made a mistake, defend it to the death. Mistakes were punished not forgiven. And love, now that *was* a shocking thought. Grown men don't need anyone to care for them, praise them or get excited by their successes. Nor should boys.

It didn't end with school. The first organizations I worked for didn't go in much for curiosity, forgiveness and love either. Procedures, reprimands and appraisal-systems were, if I remember, their preferred devices.

Thank goodness, schools and organizations are different these days, they reflect a bit more the way we learn in life. In life, learning *has* to start with curiosity. If you don't ask questions you won't get any answers, from yourself or anyone else. Think of young children, poking their noses everywhere. Lose your curiosity and you become a cabbage.

Then come the mistakes. We all make mistakes when we try something new – look at young children again. But we won't learn from them unless we can accept that they are mistakes. Punish them and we get defensive, forgive them and we can work on them. Some organizations understand this now. I asked a personnel manager how he explained the success of his development programme. 'In one word,' he said, 'forgiveness. We give them big jobs. They make mistakes. We correct them but we forgive them. They learn and grow.'

And then there's love, or what my world calls 'unconditional positive regard'. Children will accept any rebuke from someone who they know loves them to distraction. Love the sinner, hate the sin. Grown men and women are no better, we can accept a rebuke much better if it comes from someone we know cares for us, come what may. We know too that warm encouragement brings out the best in us, as does support against the odds. Unconditional positive regard! Just call it love.

I wonder now about that biblical quote, that you can't get to heaven unless you become like little children. I wonder if perhaps he isn't suggesting that the ways in which children learn should be our ways, our ways to reach our full potential, our full humanity. I wonder now why I never saw the Bible as a manual of learning theory. Curiosity, forgiveness, love – they are all there. It would be nice if they were also in the statute book!

Enterprise for What?

Britain's back in business, they say. More efficient now than West Germany at making steel, as good as the Japanese at making cars, even increasing her share of world trade again. Britain is no longer a businessman's joke, says *Fortune*, but a model of successful enterprise.

It's true. When I go to conferences of businessmen abroad they no longer smile behind their hands when the British talk. They lean forward now and listen respectfully. There's undoubtedly, too, a new self-confidence among Britain's business men and women and, yes, a new spirit of enterprise. It's true and it has to be good that it is true, because with more wealth we can do more things for more people, with more people.

But there has to be that 'because'. The wealth has to be there for a purpose. I met an Australian the other day who had come to England to escape what she saw as the crude commercialism of her own country. 'But now that Britain is going the same way,' she said, 'I might as well be materialistic in the sun!'

The poet George Oppen once put it more dramatically.
He wrote:

> Wolves may hunt
> With wolves, but we will lose
> Humanity in the cities, stores and offices
> In simple
> Enterprise

(It could almost be a trailer for that film *Wall Street*.)

Enterprise, in other words, must not stop with enterprise or we lose our humanity. And if you believe that our humanity is of a special kind, that we are here to use our talents to make a difference to this world of ours, that we are meant to stand for something not just exist, then to lose your humanity is to lose your soul.

We cannot, however, duck out of the challenge because we fear the risks; we cannot forswear enterprise, success and riches just because we might lose our way in them. No one ever said that riches were wrong, only that they made life more difficult. You have to be grown up to handle them, you have to have a purpose bigger than yourself; if, that is, your life is ever going to be more than just a set of statistics.

The individuals whom I know, who use their talents and their enterprise for purposes beyond themselves, are those whom I most admire, whether they live richly or scantily. The same goes for companies. Those who are most exciting to work for are, often, the most profitable as well. Let us hope, and let us make sure, that the next *Fortune* article on Britain applauds not only our enterprise but its purpose.

Tough Trusting

Our street, I have to tell you, is in a ferment these days. My neighbour wants to change his property, to rebuild it in fact. *He* calls the change a development and an improvement. *They* call it a disaster. The letters pouring into the planning office don't spell out, too often, quite why it would be a disaster. It is just a shame, they say, to change something that has been that way for a hundred years, even though it is falling down. Change in our street, as so often, is assumed to be change for the worse.

Yet here I am this afternoon going off to yet another management course on how to make changes happen. To those managers it will all be heady stuff, to them change is the latest 'in' word. If you aren't an agent of change these days you are nowhere. Change for them is assumed to be change for the better. Put *them*, however, at the receiving end of someone else's changes, after a takeover for instance, and you may hear another story, for change is bad change if it isn't *your* change.

Basically, I suppose, we don't like change because we don't trust other people and because we don't trust the future. My managers need to remember that; that where there is no trust there is usually no change. I would suggest however that if we *could* trust the future *and* if we could trust ourselves then those changes would not worry us. Life after all has to change. It can't be eighty years of walking on the same spot, even if it's a nice spot. That's called marking time. Life should be a journey, and because it is always a different journey for each one of us, and always has been, it is bound to be a journey into the unknown. We should not expect the maps to be good or the guides to be reliable. Nor is it a good idea to walk it looking backwards at the past.

In fact, as I get older, I know that it is from the unexpected twists and turns in life's journey that I have learnt most and that so often what looked like deviations can turn out to be the main roads. My daughter has been struck down this year by an unexplained virus. It is difficult and depressing for her, but the other day she said to me, 'Do you know, I've never noticed the spring before.' (She is twenty-three.) 'It really is quite something. If I had not been ill I would not have looked.' Starting from there she has begun to turn this particular deviation into a time of personal investment as well as sickness.

More and more, now, I begin to glimpse what Julian of Norwich, that good lady, meant so long ago by what she called God's secret, that 'all will be well and all manner of thing will be well' even if we know not how or when. That is not wishy-washy optimism, it is the kind of *tough trust* you need if you are going to make the most of your journey. 'All manner of thing will be well' – believe that and you can take change in your stride.

Negative Capability

Uncertainty, they say, is part of the human condition. I sometimes wonder, however, just how much uncertainty our human condition can stand.

I don't remember a time when the news has been so compelling, everywhere. Change is in the air, like spring – heady, and frightening. The neatest bit of news that I saw, in December 1989, when walls were falling all over Europe, was an item in the *International Herald Tribune*. '5000 Alsatian guard-dogs surplus in East Germany,' it said. 'Too violent to be used as household pets.' It was, I felt, an apt symbol of the end of the Cold War. But then I spared a thought or two for the man or woman who had had what they thought was a secure business breeding and training alsatians to prowl the wall. A nice little niche market, you might say, destroyed overnight. Change is *not* heady when it happens to you – just frightening.

Most of us therefore hope and pray that it won't happen to us. 'Why cannot the status quo be the way forward?' someone once wistfully asked. The Old Testament psalmist was more realistic: 'It is the fool and the brutish person,' he wrote, 'who in their inward thoughts think that their houses will continue for ever, their dwelling places for all generations, who call their lands after their own names.' We should be so lucky.

Product life-cycles are down to six months in some businesses. Models are out-of-date before you've read the ads. What was a meadow in January is a motorway in November. You had best assume that next year is an unsolved problem for which last year's solutions provide no help. Uncertainty, as I have said, is part of the human condition.

Another poet, Keats this time, had an answer. Negative Capability, that's what's needed he said; negative capability which he defined as when a man is capable of being in *uncertainties*, *mysteries* and *doubts*. Negative capability – the strength to keep going when all about you is in flux, when the future is a blank sheet of paper waiting for you to write on it. Let us hope that Mikhail Gorbachev has his cup flowing over with it.

Negative Capability – it's an ugly phrase for a poet to use. I prefer the pillar of cloud by day and pillar of fire by night that was God's sign of reassurance to the Israelites in the wilderness. Because that's what religion has always been about, not certainty, but the strength to live with *uncertainty*, in the wilderness, in the face of death. Negative Capability – I guess it's a jargon word for Faith.

Seven Intelligences

I was vicariously proud when my young cousin Gillian went off to St James's Palace to collect her gold award in the Duke of Edinburgh's Award Scheme. This scheme, with its emphasis on social and practical skills, on adventure and discovery, and on service to others, reminds me that not all learning takes place in the classroom. Just as well, one might think, given the worries expressed by the Chief Inspector of England's schools when he warned that the whole education service might collapse without a lot more qualified and competent teachers.

That month, too, my two-and-a-half-year-old niece was threatened with expulsion from her playgroup for demanding one-to-one attention. She will go far, that girl; but she won't get her way in English schools where soon there may not be enough teachers for one-to-fifty in some subjects.

We must heed these warnings. Surely, we must not ration learning, for God did not ration our human potential, He just calls it different names in different people. I revel in the research which has pinned down seven different types of intelligence. There's the intellectual intelligence, of course, but also the musical intelligence, the creative intelligence, the practical and the physical, the social and the psychic.

Yes, in that sense pop musicians are intelligent, so are footballers, so are those who can take a carburettor to bits and put it together again but could not spell it to save their lives. Call it talent if you prefer but I like the thought that we are all intelligent in our own way.

What is interesting is that the intelligences are not connected, so that the girl who is a dunce in class can be a wow as a bond dealer, or the expert scaffolder can be hopeless at the geometry he practises. 'Oh, he's intellectual all right,' complained my daughter of her scholarly friend, 'but practical he's not, he couldn't run a bath let alone that band of his.'

St Paul was making the same kind of point when he told the worldly-wise Corinthians that the gifts of the spirit came in different forms to different people, but all were as necessary as the different parts of the body are to health. Life would be awful if we were all the same. It's when I look around at my friends that I now realize how each of them is intelligent in their own way, although I never looked at it that way before.

To me, now, it is an article of faith that everyone is intelligent in some way. The challenge is to find the way. Some never do. They are our sadness. But for the future let us at least make sure that all our children discover that they are intelligent in their own particular way, in or out of school, before they get trapped into jobs or lives where they cannot shine. Then no one need feel stupid anymore.

The Choir of Male Convenience

When my son was young he had the dubious privilege of attending a choir school. It was dubious, I felt, because on top of all his schoolwork he had to do two and a half hours every day of music. It was hard work although he seemed to enjoy it.

After a bit I had cause to remark on a strange discrepancy in his end-of-term reports. Those from his form-master spoke of his generally disruptive behaviour, lack of concentration and apparent inability to learn. The choir-master, on the other hand, was full of praise for his diligence and hard work.

I spoke to the choir-master. What was his great secret, I asked. Did he beat them or threaten to lock them up? 'No,' he said, 'I do nothing, but I tell you what the difference is – in the choir they are doing proper work, with adults, and so they behave like adults.'

It was a message that more teachers should learn, I thought, but I went on to wonder why it was that only in a choir school do young boys get treated as men. Then I hit on it – the only thing that grown men cannot do better than small boys is to sing in a treble voice. They have to let them in on the act, and if not small boys then soprano-voiced ladies.

Choirs are the necessary exception, it seems. Everything else has, for a long time, been organized for adult male convenience. At work, it is very convenient, is it not, that one should have a work-home-from-home that requires our presence just for those forty or fifty hours when homes need cleaning and kids need caring. Inevitably it is a custom which excludes one person from that work-home and there are no prizes for guessing which that person is!

I wonder, today, how necessary it is that we should all be in the same place and all at the same time in order to get the work done. I don't wonder, actually, I know that now that most of us are assembling or processing bits of information not bits of things, it is far from essential to be all together all the time, even though we shall probably always want and need to meet our colleagues two or three times each week. You don't have to have huge office blocks full of commuters to make *that* possible. But I do wonder when we shall get round to acknowledging that a lot of that office time was always to do with male convenience. I bet that we males would not have organized things that way if it was us who had also to run a home and take the kids to school.

Ironically, I think that if we started to organize things for female convenience, with more flexibility, more control over where and when one did one's work, more personal responsibility and less minute-by-minute supervision, men might actually like it just as much as women. Well, we shall soon find out because our organizations are going to need those women more and more.

Personally, I think that organizations of male convenience have always been unnatural, in every sphere. The myth of Genesis, as I understand it, was that Adam on his own would have been a non-viable operation, or short-term at best. I still think that's true.

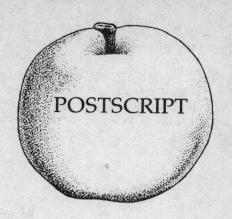

POSTSCRIPT

The Mystery of the Universe

I am no poet, but I was once asked to try my hand at poetry, to provide some of the words for a musical cantata. Here it is – the beginnings of a philosophy of religion.

There is a mystery at the heart of things.

Why don't we die?
So much of life is worry, toil and tears
Why do we strive so busily to stay alive?
Why not just die?

What is Beauty made of?
We love the beauty in a sunset, a painting or a face
We know it's beauty when we see it, but who can say
What makes it so?

And then there's Joy
How good it is to laugh, to sing, to dance,

To see the eyes of children smile – but who
Invented Joy?

There is this mystery at the heart of things

Or what of Love?
Why *should* we care for others, or put another first?
Why need the love of others to be whole ourselves?
A strange thing Love.

Whence comes our Energy?
So many strive each day to build a better world,
Putting heart and body to a stringent daily test,
Why *do* they bother?

What keeps us Good?
When the way ahead is snared with tempting traps
Like sloth and gluttony, or selfishness and greed.
Whence comes our virtue?

There is more mystery at the heart of things

Could it be chance?
We all are just a random mix of genes
Our feelings chemistry, our bodies particles in flight.
Is it all luck?

Or is there something?
Some force or reason, some point behind it all
Something that hounds us on, for each to find
A Spirit and a Truth?

Is there a mystery in the heart of things?

NOTE

The Cantata 'The Mystery of the Universe' with music by Barrie Guard, played by Andy McCullough and the Clarinet Connection, with the words narrated by Judi Dench, was published as a record by ICY Records, P.O. Box 94, SW1W 9EE in 1987.